CAREER GROWTH AND JOY AT WORK

CAREER GROWTH AND JOY AT WORK

Ashutosh Pande

genNEXT Publication

Career Growth And Joy At Work

ISBN: 978-81-80222-33-2

Published in 2011 in India by
GenNext Publications
23, Main Ansari Road,Daryaganj,
New Delhi-110002
Phones : 23282060, 23261060
Fax : 011-23285914

Lasser Type Setting by: Rudra Computer Graphics, Delhi
Printed at : Chawla Offset Press, Delhi

This book is dedicated to my parents

Contents

Contents

Preface

When I started my professional career two decades earlier there were very limited choices. In those days you could opt for being a Doctor, Engineer, Army officer or Civil Servant. Over the years the choices have increased tremendously. Not only that, it is also possible to switch careers mid way both to your personal satisfaction and for increasing your earnings. It is also possible to be in one job and have a part time business as well. These are just some of the myriad possibilities of our complex world.

Today people are experiencing a great amount of stress, which inevitably is linked to their work life. There is stress due to overwork, monotonous or boring work and lack of new skills. There is stress because we find that our skills are becoming obsolete. There is also stress due to lack of work and not enough career prospects. On one hand there are lot of new career opportunities and avenues coming up in our new growth economy, but there are no "footprints" of experienced professionals to guide us.

The scenario though good for us is also causing confusion in young and old both. It is difficult to decide as to what is good for us. How to prepare ourselves to career opportunities that are in line with our aptitudes, values and temperament, while also being flexible to explore new emerging possibilities without being constrained by set beliefs about what everybody seem to be doing. This book is about building an enriching and motivating environment around us that makes it possible to develop our winning strategies around our strengths.

Basically, I have adapted the concepts of management being practiced in the corporate world- motivation, creative thinking, strategic thinking etc to an Individual's concern for career growth & joy at work. However these concepts and techniques are adapted and simplified in a jargon free manner and are easily understandable to anyone who is mature and serious about his or her career.

It will help you in visualizing and reflecting on your strengths and key advantages for working out your unique strategy of career growth and joy at work. You will be able to open new avenues for your personal growth as well as career advancement by designing your Generic project that will help you in being flexible and responsive to ever new opportunities apart from your present occupation be it as a student, professional or experienced executive.

The book which is written like a companion guide will also provide useful concepts, tools, and exercises for strengthening key competencies, self-branding and positioning yourself vis-a vis your competitors to gain a competitive edge over others. Finally and most importantly it will tell you how to plan and execute the quantum leap with precision and right timing. So go on and make the best use of this companion guide.

All the best for a fruitful and joyful Career!
Author

For Whom This Book is

The changing work scenario does provide a lot of promise to the young and dynamic but at the same time there is total dearth of guidance for understanding the cacophony of countless new opportunities and the type of jobs which our parents had never heard of. For example jobs like radio jockey, dance therapist, marine biotechnologist were completely unknown a few years ago. This book therefore serves as the right starting point for any one who wishes to understand the implication of all these new possibilities in light of his own potential. More specifically this book is likely to be of immense help to:

1. People who wish to energies their working life and develop their career for happiness and all round growth.

2. People who wish to improve their career prospects and wish to transform their old career to the needs of the new economy.

3. People who have lost the passion in their job and need to redesign their career for their mental and better physical health.

4. Parents of youngsters who need to guide their children and act as role model to inspire their children in the right direction in line with their aptitude and interests.

5. People who wish to develop careers which are essentially a part time job

6. Youngsters who are planning or pursuing professional courses seeking new employment.

7. People who wish to discover their inner "calling" and link it up with their everyday life.

Objectives

This book will enable you to:

- Understanding your unique strengths, aptitude, and resources for career growth and advancement.
- Find new avenues and opportunities through your generic project apart from your present occupation as a student, professional or experienced executive etc.
- Master necessary skills for self-branding and positioning and making the most of upcoming opportunities in your field.
- Plan and execute the quantum leap in your career growth with a calibrated precision.

Acknowledgements

This book would not have been possible without the direct and indirect support of several persons. The initial ideas about this book germinated when I was working as Consultant with National Productivity Council. Those were the days of frequent travel and tours, which provided ample opportunities to visit various places in India and abroad.

Idyllic discussions with professionals from several fields have helped shape my ideas gradually over a period of time. Numerous interactions with my colleagues and participants of my programs at Power Management Institute, (NTPC), Noida has further nourished these ideas in the last few years.

I am especially thankful to the lush green and serene environment of Power Management Institute and its learning culture which has encouraged me to think in new and creative ways while writing this book.

My special thanks to my father in law Late Sh. R.C.Pant, Retired Principle, for contributing real life experiences and anecdotes from his work life, which find a place in this book.

Finally, I am thankful to my Parents and family members for providing all the support and encouragement for completing this book in time.

Ashutosh Pande

How to Get the Best Out of this Book

This book is neither like a story book nor a very serious one, proffering loads of directions and advice. It is more like a companion guide which encourages and challenges you to experiment with innovative ideas and novel approaches for career growth and joy at work.

This is like a companion guide, intended to be your life partner forever! It is intended to be a constant source of Vision, inspiration and learning to make the best of your inherent strengths and the new and emerging opportunities of our ever-changing world.

What is more it will provide you with ample tools and exercises to enable you to harness the best of your experience for crafting your own strategies of career growth and joy at work. It will also enable you to make a switch over to a new growth area, if you need to.

The really important parts of this book are the tools and exercises aimed for working out your own generic project around your key strengths and resources. For best results use a pencil and paper when you do the exercises and apply the tools to your specific situation and then keep a brief record for your future reference in your daily dairy, other wise you may simply photocopy the relevant pages and keep the filled in record with you. This will help you in mapping your own progress through your development Phase and work out appropriate action points and goals. At the end of the companion guide there is a section on Action Planning so that you can use the learning and integrate the same in your actual work setting as well as share your learning and insights with friends and well wishers. A list of career resources including useful books, journals, websites etc is also provided at the end.

Networking for support

The best results will come when you discuss some of your career concerns and issues with counselors, trustworthy friends and/or well-wishers etc. During the course of working through this book, you may come to know of the strengths and special aptitudes of some other friends of yours.

It is also possible that there is similarity in the nature of problems or issues that you are facing in your day-to-day working. The profile of such friends and/or colleagues as well as any other professional or expert, networking with whom may be helpful for your growth development may be noted in the format given below.

List of Resource Persons

Sl. No.	*Name*	*Areas of Strength / Mutual Interests*	*Contact details*	*Email*

(Contd.)

(Contd. Table)

Sl. No.	Name	Areas of Strength / Mutual Interests	Contact details	Email

1

Introduction

Musings for a Dream Career

If you cant laugh while you work and smile while you toil

If you cant act while you think and think while you act

If you find yourself drifting aimlessly and always short of time

If you find that your goals come from others.

When you begin your day with priorities but cant keep to them

When work is always a hard toil to be endured.

Then, is it not the time to stop! Take a breadth and begin a new journey where work, self and relationships are all combined into a meaningful melody of your own composition.

A melody of soul and of mind, a melody which makes the journey joyful and weaves your self and career into a meaningful purpose of your own inner calling.

Amidst this cacophony of competition and mindless rat race, would you not like to compete with yourself to realize your true potential through your work and career in ways that are worldly and in ways that are beyond.

The Purpose of Work Life or Career

As a trainer and consultant it was intriguing to see how some people always seemed to be motivated and energized while they came for work day after day. These people weren't necessarily the part of top management team or some IIT pass outs etc, but they came from all strata of the organization. As I once said to a colleague of mine, it appeared that they all came to work riding a "Cycle of Passion" and went back home the same way.

These people to my eye seem to be climbing the Ladder of happiness and satisfaction every day of their life. They were deriving satisfaction and growth from their work and to a great extent the work itself had become a source of growth and happiness for them. As a trainer I also saw a vast majority of people who simply seem to be carrying their jobs as drudgery, something that they have to do to eak out a living. These other groups of people were those who always dreamt of doing something worthwhile, while outside their job. Many of them had great plans after retirements or after office hours but work for them was essentially a boring daily grind, which had to be endured for the sake of earning a livelihood.

In today's world people are spending more and more of their time at work and what happens to them during the work situation cast a powerful shadow in their personal lives also. For those who are not working, the same analogy can be applied to whatever productive work they are carrying out as part of their present role-such as studies, house work, any business, part time work, looking for job etc. Having observed this work-happiness association in many successful people and from my own experience also I have realized that we tend to be our best when we are riding this "cycle of passion", which is all within us.

If we can create the same cycle of passion in every individual, then their will be no dearth of talent for any kind of job and work will itself become the source of happiness, health and wealth for everybody. Often times discovering this cycle of passion is like understanding your own self and at the same time it is also about how you wish to see your work. The work can thus become a constant source of happiness and growth.

What should be the ultimate purpose of our work life or career? Should it be money, growth, status, happiness or can we think of something else beyond all this. Now, what would you say if you are told that the ultimate purpose of our work life is achieving tranquility of mind? Many people would find it difficult to even think of tranquility of mind in the context of their work situation. For many people Work, Tasks, Career are all words that are synonymous of hard toil which has to be endured for the sake of earning a living. How could work bring peace of mind in itself? For many the real solace and the peace of mind comes from something outside of the chaotic and turbulent world of work-perhaps a hobby or religion etc. So we fragment life in different compartments – a compartment of work and a compartment of joy. A compartment to learn and a compartment to play, a time to toil and a time to rest and so on till there isn't enough in each compartment!

Career Growth and Tranquility of Mind

"One route to more happiness is called flow' an engrossing state that comes during creative or playful activities"

- Mihaly Csikszentmihalyi in his book Flow: The psychology of optimal experience.

People in the "flow" create a mental state that brings them peace and fulfilment that does not depend on their environment. Many creative people- artist, authors as well as spiritual gurus experience this feeling, when they are immersed in their work. These are moments when you are completely absorbed in some activity and experience a loss of awareness about your surroundings. You can develop the capacity of engaging in flow experience by learning to match your personal strength with the task at hand. When you continue to experience this flow state day after day and are able to look forward to your career and work as a source of it, you are able to develop a tranquil mind.

A Tranquil mind is one that is calm and quite and is able to concentrate on real and important issue for prolonged period of time to find unique solutions to everyday problem of our existence. Such a mind is uniquely endowed with the capability of responding appropriately to everyday challenges of our work and life. In the context of career growth, tranquillity of mind is utmost important because of two reasons;

- Only a calm and tranquil mind can take right decision after considering the pros and cons of all options available.

- Only a tranquil mind can be able to take the challenge of our competitive times in right stride and enjoy the journey which is so essential for maintaining a healthy balance.

Taking a different perspective, we can say that we have a better chance of achieving tranquility of mind only when we are able to plan and manage our career well. Not being able to plan and manage our career well often leads to sense of frustration and desperation. This soon erodes the confidence and sense of self worth, thus affecting other aspects of our life. Even if we wish to enjoy a hobby or a favorite passion peacefully, we need to be confident and relaxed that our career is taking a satisfactory shape.

If we look deeply we will find that concepts and approaches for career management provides an excellent ground not only for earning a living but also to develop a tranquil, calm and concentrated mind that helps in realizing our true potential in work situation. Mastering the necessary skills and making the most of upcoming opportunities will help us in becoming more resilient to the competitive pressures of modern times.

The path ahead

Many people think that choosing a career mean choosing a job or profession. But choosing a career is much more than that. Career means a path through which you plan your own growth and progress over a period of time. In that sense career is important for everyone whether you are in a job, or you are a student, businessman, homemaker etc.

In our society the term career is often used to indicate some kind of paid work such as earning through work or business. This is so because most people spend a major part of their life engaged is some economic activity or working in some capacity. The type of work you do helps you build an identity for yourself. The type of career you choose has an important influence in your overall personality, lifestyle and other social aspects also. Successfully integrating work in your life is an important aspect of fitting into society and maintaining good mental health. People face career choices through out their active life. These choices may involve enrolling for educational course, a professional degree, getting a job, part time work, doing an internship or part time project, starting a business or changing job etc.

Technological advances have opened up new opportunities both in terms of more types of jobs as well as more flexible ways of doing work. By taking an active interest in managing your career you can be truly empowered to take the right decision at the right time and reap the benefits of a booming economy as well as derive personal satisfaction. This book has three main themes:

A Mental Model which Helps in Discovering and Nurturing Our Inherent Strengths

This part is about developing a Resilient mindset- a mind that is capable of thriving under pressure and is aimed at building a rock solid foundation for empowering self through positive beliefs and developing a mind set for generating quality choices and decisions.

A Vision Based on our Inherent Strengths and Emerging Career Opportunities

The most important parts of this book, it comprises of tools and exercises aimed for working out our own generic project around our key strengths and resources. Using these exercises readers will design their own Generic project (GP) as vehicle for developing the competencies in a broad area of interest, which is of great importance for long-term career prospects.

Execution-The Art of Making it Happen

This part talks about how to link everyday work and career aspects to your inner calling, thus enabling you to gravitate to the kind of job or profession which is best suited for career growth as well as personal satisfaction. There are exercises to understand one's aptitude and interest and craft career strategies accordingly for optimizing career growth and joy at work. This includes advancing your present career as well as switching career to more rewarding ones.

Some Career Vocabulary and their Usage in the Book

It would be worthwhile to take a note of meaning of some of the common terms which we shall be using in the book.

Work: Is a goal directed activity for achieving some objectives. Though work is generally differentiated from play, or leisure, yet there are cases where the distinction may not be very obvious. For e.g a professional cricket player may consider playing cricket as work or profession, whereas for most of us it may be a playful activity. It is generally believed that when engaged in play or leisure a person has a greater autonomy regarding the outcomes of the activity. Work on the other hand implies achieving a particular outcome or result.

Skills: Work related knowledge, and capability which is developed through education, training and experience which is required to perform well in particular types of jobs. Sometimes the same skills may be helpful in doing different types of work, jobs or businesses. Even a skill picked up as a result of a hobby may be useful in getting some work or part time job in a organization. For e.g a dancer may help corporate executives in managing stress through evening classes of dance therapy. Similarly a lady with excellent skills in microwave cooking may be hired for running demonstration classes for new buyers. Such skills which can be transferred from one work situation to other are called transferable skills and may help in widening the scope of one's career choices.

Position: Is the formal place in an organizational chart which represents the reporting relationship and responsibilities of the incumbent at that position. Normally when organizations plan to add to its work force, it recruits people against the positions for which there is need or where there is a vacancy due to retirement or resignation etc. However not all organization fill all the available positions. It is very much possible for a position to include part of duties of a single job or it may encompass duties of multiple jobs also. Over a period of time organizations are restructured, old positions are abolished and new positions are created. Sometime it is also possible to create a new position to accommodate a talented person whose need is being felt in the organization.

Job: In common parlance people use the term job and position to mean the same. However job is a broader term that includes the duties and responsibilities of similar positions across different work situations. A job represents the basic set of skills and experience which qualifies a person to apply for similar positions. For e.g. when a person applies for a job, he applies to several employers who are seeking an employee for their specific position. The same basic skill set of the job may qualify the person to be considered for different positions by different employers or even for winning a contract or starting a business successfully.

Role: Is the set of expectations that other people have from an incumbent occupying a particular position. These could further qualify the duties and responsibilities of a job or position. Role is more dynamic in nature and includes the expectations of customers, suppliers, colleagues, boss and subordinates. While the duties and responsibilities may remain broadly the same there may be some requirement born out of the expectations of others who work alongside the incumbent. For e.g. in a company which has started loosing young talent frequently, it may be expected of the boss to make special efforts to counsel, mentor and reward talented employee so that talent is retained and not lost to the competitors. When other roles outside the work situation strengthen each other, a person may experience more harmony and satisfaction in his career.

Generic Project (GP): The long term project which you constantly look forward to returning and which gives you a constant purpose and focus and which is not necessarily depended on a particular desk or a position you occupy but is rather something more enduring – something which arises out of the inner calling but gets a concrete shape after mulling over the world of external opportunities and the cues that they provide to you.

Career: According to oxford English dictionary Career is a term defined - as an individual's "course or progress through life (or a major part of life)". It usually is considered to pertain to paid work or employment.

In its most common usage it is often referred to as series of jobs or positions held by an individual. However, as the idea of self direction and personal choice is gaining ground in recent times, there is increased acceptance of people having multiple kinds of work. The idea of a career is therefore shifting from a given set of achievements, like a chronological resume of past jobs, to a meaningful set of pursuits looking forward. In its broadest sense, career refers to an individual's work and life roles over their entire lifespan.

Career Growth: Career growth refers to the process which helps you integrate work and life roles in a manner to get the best out of various career opportunities, while also experiencing the joy of contributing meaningfully to the society and deriving overall satisfaction from your life.

2

Mental Models for Higher Latitudes

Introduction

In the game of cricket the batsman's chances of scoring high runs depends, to a great extent on the choices of stroke available to him. A player who is equally at ease playing on front foot, back foot, off side, on side and so on has a greater chance to withstand different types of bowling attacks. Similarly our ability to generate quality choices makes all the difference in achieving success in our work or career.

In the last few years the world of work has undergone a complete transformation. Career fields which were sought after are no longer attractive, however many new career fields have emerged with exciting possibilities. Concept of Boundary-less careers coupled with knowledge explosion and technological development are creating new avenues and exciting possibilities unheard of before.

On one hand we are constantly bombarded by so much information about fresh avenues for the young aspirants, on the other hand there is "metamorphosis of old careers", redefining new career opportunities for experienced professionals. No wonder it is easily possible to get confused with unlimited and relentless offers and opportunities. However despite all this confusion, we must be able to recognize the inflection point –when a timely initiative on our part will lead to a quantum leap in terms of achieving what we want. Our success will depend on our ability to develop new and creative goals. Search for innovative ways of achieving career growth would also mean constantly reevaluating our needs for balancing between work and family.

More and more in times to come, we would need the skills to be resilient in times of change. The future will demand from us many new skills-art of taking risk, be willing to change, moving to a new field etc. We will need to adjust to the new and uncertain nature of loyalty from and to Organization. All this will make it necessary for us to be able to find ways to deal with feelings of discontent and rather use our emotions in positive manner.

Our success in times of change will depend on how we perceive "the world of work" and how we feel about it. Do we get completely overwhelmed by fast changes and drown ourselves in despair or we take this as an opportunity to make the most of it. The ways in which we perceive and understand our work and environment will shape our mental models, which in turn are guided by our values, beliefs and experiences. Understanding and developing our mental models will help us in developing quality choices and aligning our thoughts and feeling for achieving the desired success. So, let us start the journey by creating a powerful process of self-empowerment. Self empowerment involves taking a stock of our internal resources- our mental models and thinking patterns that are always within us. This process is something similar to the way you check items in your baggage before embarking on a long journey.

Begin the journey with self exploration

"What lies behind us and what lies before us are small matters compared to what lies within us." — Ralph Waldo Emerson... American Scholar

Though self-exploration is a vast subject including spiritual aspects of life, however, self-exploration in the limited context of this book simply means an open-minded enquiry to draw inspiration and insights from the powerful reservoir of our latent potential, which is not readily visible to us in the rig morale of our daily life.

The process should also help us in reflecting on our unique gifts, then develop, and use this knowledge through out our journey

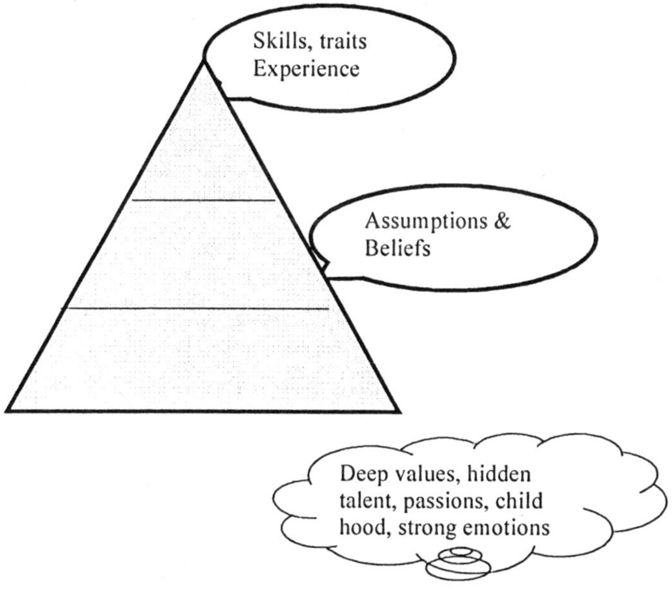

Fig 2.1 Levels of Self-Exploration

of career growth and learning for practical applications in our work life.

As in an iceberg, what is latent or hidden is much more than what is visible. We need to explore this latent aspect of our personality. This exploration is extremely useful in understanding our latent potential.

In the iceberg diagram shown above the visible part represents our skills, experience, known motives, etc about ourselves, however much of our resources such as Values, beliefs are below the surface. What is readily observable in terms of skills, traits, experience etc get a new meaning when we also understand our deep values, latent passions and talents etc. These hidden resources are like unpolished gems. This fascinating journey of self-exploration will show you many such latent treasures waiting to be discovered and polished.

As you can see in this diagram these resources can be very diverse-Deep rooted Values, deep desires or feelings, a lost interest, childhood fantasy or pangs etc. This journey will help you discover some of these and apply it for your own career growth.

If you love yourself- Set yourself free (of any biases, prejudices etc)

I am reminded of a story of a naturalist who once saw an eagle brought up along side chickens and decided to set the mighty eagle free to fly in the boundless sky. The story goes something like this. An eagle brought up along with chickens in a farm house develops all the traits of chickens and behaves like one. It could not even learn to fly like an eagle. Thanks to the intervention of the naturalist-the eagle was able to discover its true potential. The naturalist gave the right opportunity to the eagle and set it free so that it could fly and explore the boundless sky.

Many of us are in a similar situation. We are in cages of different kinds. How do we set our self-free? We may say that we need to have an understanding of our self so that we can know our strengths, weaknesses and our potential. But even before we do that we need to set ourselves free, otherwise we may tend to conclude what we have been told by our boss or parents or authority figures and we may never challenge our way of seeing the potential within us.

Ask Questions to Yourself with Child Like Curiosity

The veil of ignorance can only be removed by asking the right questions to self. However, when a person puts certain questions to himself, the answers he gets also depend largely on his initial assumptions or beliefs that are in his mind while asking that question. It is something similar to what happens in science – if your initial assumptions about the problem you are investigating are incorrect then what you are going to build upon, will also be completely meaningless. We need to ask our self various questions- questions regarding our unique strengths etc, but with what belief we ask this questions is of great importance for our constant quest for illuminating our understand of the vast potential that is hidden beneath us.

As shown in the fig 2.2, we need to start the process of self-introspection or analysis with a positive belief about our self and then try to get the answers. If I may draw an analogy with a computer, we may say that, if a virus corrupts the software, the result will be trash however advanced is the computer. Similarly however intelligent or competent you are, but if your own basic assumption or belief about your self are incorrect then this entire journey of self exploration will be a complete waste of time.

Sometime life's bitter experience can make a person loose faith in everything around him. For some persons the cumulative effect of many a bad experience is such that they are at a stage of

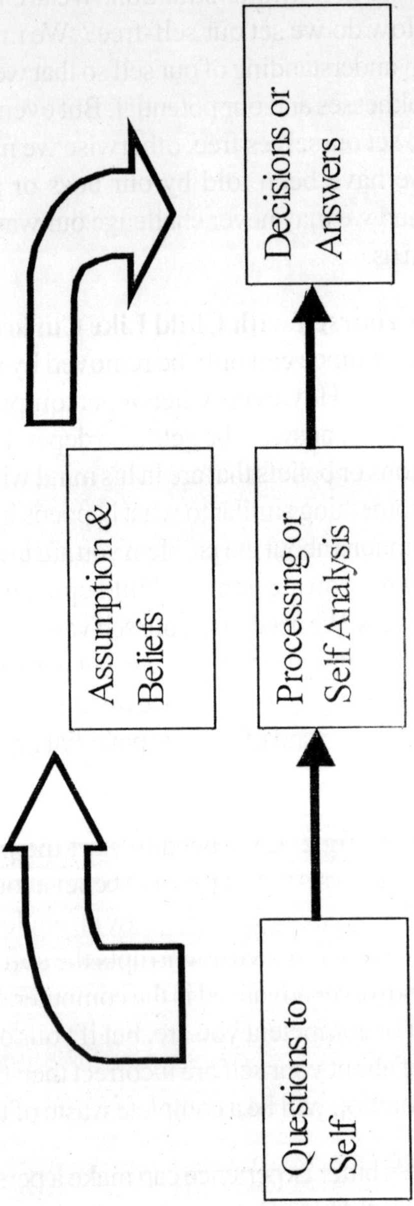

Fig. 2.2 Assumptions and Beliefs Supporting Self Introspeclion

–1 all the time, so if they have to come to the positive belief stage of +1 then they must necessarily pass through the 0 stage.

There is an interesting story of a professor going to a Zen master to learn something about Zen. By the time professor introduces himself to the Zen master by telling him all his achievements, degrees etc, tea arrives. Zen master pours the tea while the professor is speaking. The professor is astonished to see that the tea has started overflowing the saucer, yet the Zen master continues to pour the tea. So, he interrupts –what are you doing sir the tea is spilling all over? Zen master replies- Just like no further tea can be accommodated in this over flowing saucer; similarly, it is not possible to give you any new learning, since you are so full of your own ideas etc.

Being in Zero state refers to the tendency of being free of any biases or prejudices, when exploring our true potential. This simple story reveals the importance of the Zero state for any body who wish to discover his latent potential and polish it further. This state is important if you are not satisfied with your success in life. It is also important if you are fully satisfied with whatever is your success in life.

Developing an "Oasis of Faith" within Oneself

Basic approach is very simple. You begin by involving yourself in some activity, which is new to you, about which you do not have any preset notions. It could be a physical activity like jogging, swimming, Gym or Yoga or even a mental activity like playing chess, solving puzzles etc. Alternatively, just take up something where you have the genuine humility to accept that you know very little about it. The activity is just a means of experiencing your self in a fresh way rather than the stereotyped manner in which you could be treating yourself. It is just a tool to help you come out of the "inertia" of your present state, which could be bothering you.

You could have been in a spiral of experience, which has led to building a negative mindset. The basic idea of the approach is that you experience something different for about a month. You will come to the Zero state when you start experiencing the positive energy around you. The activity may be small or big or even small ritual, but may be done in nice environment. It is preferable if it could be done with a group of people who are themselves positive and successful. So just, start with any positive activity or ritual like jogging or praying or yoga or any other hobby of your choice.

Let your mind come to each aspect of your belief after you have experienced this zero activity for about a week. Question yourself on each aspect of your belief (which has been bothering you) after that zero activity, introspects and ask yourself the questions, whether it is good to believe like this. Remember there is nothing right or wrong with the beliefs they are just the starting points.

We shall be returning to the questions of beliefs with particular reference to career and work later. However, let us now look at another hidden gem stone- emotions and what we can do to polish it and convert it into a powerful force.

Self Empowerment though Emotional Competence

Before we go deep into it let us see what some great minds have said about Reasoning v/s emotions and feelings

- And certainly we should take care not to make intellect our god; it has of course, powerful muscles but no personality. It can not lead; it can only serve; the intellect has a sharp eye for methods and tools, but it is blind to ends and values.

  Einstein

- .... It is the heart that takes one to the highest place, where intellect can never reach. It goes beyond intellect and reaches what is called inspiration.

  Swami Vivekanand

- And.... I know that ultimately one is guided not only by the intellect but by the heart. The heart accepts a conclusion for which the intellect subsequently finds reasoning. Arguments follow convictions. Man often finds reason in support of whatever he does or wants to do.

  Mahatma Gandhi

- ...Human reason is very convenient and accommodating instrument and works only in circle set for it by interest, partiality and prejudice.

  Sri Aurobindo

Success in Life is not dependent on your intelligence

It has been proved repeatedly that scholastic abilities and high marks in school do not guarantee success in life. There are many examples of successful entrepreneurs, managers and people from all walks for life who were neither very bright in studies nor had very high IQ. They achieved extraordinary success due to some other qualities they had. So let us look at these qualities.

Studies have shown that IQ Contributes no more than 10% to your Success in Life

Even though a high IQ is no guarantee of success in career and life, our schools, institutions and culture give a lot of importance to academic competence. They neglect emotional competence, an ability that is of enormous importance to our personal well being and success in career and life.

Just like mathematics, logic, language or science, mastering emotions and social skills can be learnt. It is important and, indeed, necessary, to know a person's emotional competence in order to understand why someone with a certain IQ has progressed in life, whilst someone else with a similar IQ has not succeeded that well. Managing emotions is vital for making the most of the journey in your career and all aspects of your life. Some authors call this quality as emotional intelligence (EI) but I prefer to call it emotional competence (EC) because the term EI gives an impression that just like IQ this is something, which is inborn and cannot be cultivated further. Emotional competence on the other hand can be developed through effort etc.

EC is a special capacity, which determines how well we are able to make use of the other skills we possess. A great deal of evidence shows that people with good emotional and social capacity – who know their feelings well, are in control of them and can read other people's feelings and deal with them effectively – have an advantage in most aspects of their personal and professional life.

Bringing Passion to your Work and Career

The achievements of, families, groups, institutions and the society at large are dependent on the commitment of each member. For many of us it is a dream to work in an environment where people are fully committed and passionate about their work. It is not only the organization which will benefit from people doing their best, but everyone will be better off trying to do their best with utmost commitment.

Deep inside, people want to give their best in their work and career, because when they bring out their best, they become proud of themselves. Pride leads to higher self-esteem and a richer life. Therefore, all stakeholders of the organization should share a vision of having deeply committed employees who bring their hearts to work. In order to make this "dream" come true it may be helpful to create such environment where everyone brings out their best and finds it natural to do so.

The Outward Success is Created in the Silent World within Self.

Our thought patterns and emotions inside create the foundations of our outward success. There is an interesting anecdote about Edison, which illustrates this point. When Edison was presenting his discovery of the electric bulb to a group of journalist, one journalist asked him –Is it not surprising that we could know the secret of making this electric bulb in 10 minutes, where as it took you so many years to discover it. Edison replied 'yes that's true but there is a difference –You know only the one correct way in which the bulb can be made, whereas I know 1464 other methods by which electric bulb can not be made. This story illustrates the importance of patience and perseverance in achieving our goals. There are some emotions, which help us to function effectively. There are also emotions that hinder us from functioning effectively. How we harness our emotions for our own growth and development is very important. The challenge is how to prevent unwanted emotions without suppressing them.

How not to be Disrupted by Unwanted Emotions?

One of the most unwanted and common emotion that disrupts our behavior is anger. So Let us take a look at this. Anger is a strong, complex, emotional and biological reaction that happens when we feel: frustrated, threatened, endangered, intimidated or hurt.

When we are angry, our bodies, minds, and emotions respond in a manner as if our survival is threatened. This response is our instinctive reaction to a threat or danger. Any stimulus that we perceive as threatening to our survival causes our whole being to go into survival mode and this simulates a fight, flight or fright response. The intensity of this response will depend on how serious we perceive the danger to be.

The Fight Response

When we feel an impulse to fight, blood flows to our arms and hands as if getting ready to grasp a weapon or launch a strike.

Our pulse rate increases and the rush of hormones generate a burst of energy for rapid and vigorous action. The tone and tenor of our voices also become louder and more threatening. Many a time such an outburst leads to irreparable loss of relationship with boss, spouse or colleague etc. When such anger continues for a long time it often changes form such as Anger leading to frustration then despair and depression. This leads to stress and bad health in the long run.

The flight response

When we want to avoid the get away from the cause of anger, blood moves to the larger muscle groups of our legs. This makes it easier for us to run. This often leads to lack of confidence and avoidance of challenge. The repeated flight response often leads to dull, cold disillusionment about people, work, career and life in general. It can thus lead to depression in the long run.

The fright response

The fright response paralyzes us. Since the blood is shunted away from our faces, we typically become pale when frightened. Even the fright response had survival value in the prehistoric times. The sudden freezing could help in avoiding the attention of predators. People can sometime become so frightened that they faint feel nausea or sudden tremors. Mentally, fright creates a blank mind where we just cannot think of a response and just freeze!

In prehistoric times our survival depended on these responses of fight, flight and fright; however these responses are not appropriate for dealing with modern day work and other conflicts. Today, the dangers we face are less explicit. But the way we react is pretty much the same. We all get angry from time to time. There would hardly be a person who doesn't get angry but how we manage our anger will impact on our long-term health and shape our career, success and personal relationships. Please take this exercise to improve your ability to respond better to an unwanted feeling at the work place.

Exercise: Discarding Unhelpful beliefs and negative emotions

Think of a disturbing situation you have experienced in the last 10-15 days or so. Briefly describe the situation in terms of what happened, who was involved, what were the unpleasant feelings and accompanying behavior etc.

Instructions:

(1) Now write down what your unpleasant feelings were and what behaviors accompanied them.

(2) Now try to capture that inner self-talk and the inner thoughts triggered by the unpleasant event. See if you can pin down what went on in your mind right after the activating event.

(3) Your next task is to actively question, dispute and discard these maladaptive, self-defeating beliefs that give rise to your Negative self-talk. Submit every element of your internal monologue to rigorous examination. Ask yourself the following key questions and write down your answers.

(a) Where is the evidence that what I am thinking is the only plausible explanation?

(b) Could there be alternative, more reasonable explanations to explain the activating event?

(c) If my advice is sought by someone regarding such a situation, what could I say that could help alter his/her perspective?

(4) This exercise will enable you to experience how the process of open minded questioning, reviewing and discarding unhelpful emotions has shifted your understanding and belief about the activating event and consequently your feelings and behaviors.

(5) How can you apply this in your work relationships and career situations?

Explore your values; what is that which gives meaning to my life

Another important aspect of self-exploration is our values. Values represent what we consider truly important and precious in our lives. If someone asks you –what are your values? Chances are that you will find it extremely difficult to think of an answer. This is because most of the times we are not conscious of our values. Though our values affect our decisions and behavior, yet we are rarely aware of them.

Values are deeply held views, of what we find worthwhile. They come from many sources: parents, religion, schools, peers, people we admire, and culture. Many go back to childhood; we take on others as adults. As with all mental models, there's a distinction between our "espoused" values-, which we profess to believe in, and our "values in action", which actually guide our behavior. These latter values are coded into our brains at such a fundamental levels that we can't easily see them. We rarely bring them to the surface or question them. That's why they create dissonance for us.

As literature and spiritual guides warn us repeatedly, individuals should beware of the temptation to let their values slip when times get tough. One good way to bring your Values to surface is to think of a story or incident that you find very inspiring. Then examine theses stories/incidents to find out what exactly is the issue or aspect due to which you find this story very inspiring. This quality or aspect which is the source of inspiration for you is likely to be your cherished value.

You can also take the exercise given below to help you reach a better understanding of your values.

Exercise: My Most Significant Values

This exercise is designed to help you understand your most significant values.

Step 1: "What I value most"

From this list of values (both work and personal), select the ten that are most important to you- as guides for how to behave, or as components of a valued way of life. Feel free to add any values of your own to this list.

Adventure	Friendship	Physical Challenge
Affection (love and caring)	Gratitude	Enjoyment
Aesthetic sense	Growth	Power and authority
Appreciation for beauty	Helping other people	Privacy
Being with my family	Music	Public service
Challenging problems	Honesty	Cleanliness
Change and variety	Independence	Innovation
Close relationships	Influencing others	Quality
Community	Inner harmony	Recognition
Competence	Integrity	Speed in work
Competition	Intellectual status	Religion
Cooperation	Involvement	Reputation
Country	Peaceful Job	Responsibility
Creativity	Knowledge	Security
Confidence	Leadership	Self-respect
Democracy	Loyalty	Sophistication

(Contd.)

(Contd. Table)

Environmental concern	Market position	Stability
Effectiveness	Meaningful work	Status
Efficiency	Merit	Supervising others
Ethics in everyday life	Money	Time freedom
Excellence	Nature	Truth
Excitement	Openness and honest	Wealth
Expertise	Order and Stability	Wisdom
Fame	Personal development (living up to the fullest use of my potential)	Work under pressure
Fast paced living	Profit	Work with others
Freedom	Peace	Working alone
Financial security	Preferred place of stay	Worship

Step 2: Articulation

Take a look at the top three values on your list.

1. What do these values mean to you? What are you expecting from yourself-even in bad times?

2. How would your life be different if you could practice these values?

3. What would an organization be like which encouraged employees to live up to those values?

4. Do your dreams and long term goals reflect those values? If not, should you revisit your dreams? Or are your prepared to reconsider your values?

5. Are you willing to choose a life, career, job or an organization, in which these values are paramount?

Step 3 : Value clarification Process

A strong value is something, which will withstand the test of time. Your strong values are reflected in what you tend to choose yourself from among the available options. You feel proud about it and base your decisions and actions on it. Your values also serve as principles based on which you tend to judge the merit of things and people. Let us now examine our strong values through the exercise given below.

Write 1 or 2 key reminders words in answer to each statement below.

(a) One thing I am proud of...

(b) I can sacrifice a lot for this.......................................

(c) When I see this quality in someone I feel emotionally so close to that person, as if.......................................

(d) This quality is so important for a happy and meaningful life.........

(e) Something I did in the past and yearn to be able to do again.........

(f) Something difficult I'm glad I did it ....
....

(g) Something I learnt to do and I feel so proud of it...

Now, for each of the response (a to g) in the step 1 above, answer the following questions honestly.

1. Have I chosen this freely and consciously from among many other alternatives?
2. Did I consider each alternative carefully before choosing this one?
3. Do I feel proud that I chose this over other alternative?
4. Have I shared this to my near and dear ones?
5. Do I consciously spent time on this or act on this?

Out of above responses (a to g) in step 1, those responses for which you have maximum "Yes" in step 2 are likely to represent some of your strongest values.

Now describe the value in your own words and answer the question below

1. How did I acquire this value
2. Since when this value is with me
3. What are the consequence of choosing this value
4. When did I last act on this Value
5. In what ways this value has become a part of my life
6. When did I talk about it to my near and dear ones or to my friends etc.
7. How do I rejoice or celebrate this Value
8. How does this value help me to grow as a person

9. In what ways this value is important for achieving career growth and joy at work.

How Helpful are your Beliefs and Emotions for Your Career Growth?

Having explored the inner world of your values and emotions, let us now take up this exercise to examine how helpful our beliefs and emotions are for career growth. Here are certain beliefs which tend to govern out emotions and mental patterns. These are not religious beliefs but "way of life" ones. Some of them you may not believe at all. Others you may strongly believe. Yet others you may only partially or moderately believe.

Directions: Go through the following checklist as honestly as you can, check marking (tick) the fill in lines before the beliefs you hold and crossing (X) the ones you don't agree with.

For best results, check or cross each item even if it is only marginally one way or the other for you.

I believe:

1.	It is inevitable that certain things at workplace would make me angry.
2.	Suppressing bad feelings is stressful and would affect performance.
3.	I can't control how I feel; my emotions just happen to me.
4.	I get mad when things go wrong and my plans are upset.
5.	Emotions are mostly a hindrance to achieving Career growth.
6.	My self-esteem largely depends on my reputation with other professional in my career field.
7.	Comparisons with other colleagues more successful than me make me feel inadequate.
8.	It is possible to prevent myself from having "bad" emotions such as anxiety, worry, anger, and guilt.
9.	I expect that others should always be polite and considerate towards me.

(Contd.)

(Contd. Table)

10.	Most of my emotions have been learned from experience.
11.	Anxiety about performance or achieving something is detrimental to my growth.
12.	Other people make me feel upset /angry irritated, etc.
13.	If I have done something wrong or dishonest, I should feel guilty about it.
14.	It is usually best to express my feelings openly and honestly, even if doing so risks offending or upsetting somebody.
15.	How I perceive events and other people's behaviour triggers my emotions.
16.	When I feel upset, I have chosen to react in this way.
17.	It is not possible to practice truly, what I value in life
18.	It is natural that my day-to-day priorities will take precedence on what I consider personally meaning full in life.
19.	My choices are restricted due to early decisions in my career
20.	Career change in my age is unthinkable

Scoring Key:

Score each belief statement using the following marking system, individually and then total your score. The highest you can get is 100. A score more than 80 is very good. 60-80 fall in the average zone and below 60 are low.

Belief Statements	*Points for checks*	*Points for crosses*
2,8,10,15,16	5	0
4,5,9,12,	0	5
1,3,6,7,11,13,14,17,18, 19,20	1	5

Interpretations

- Higher the scores, the more positive are your beliefs for managing and responding to feelings regarding career growth
- Examine unhelpful beliefs i.e. items were your scores are low. How it has come that way

- Discuss with friends/ colleagues etc and re-examine unhelpful beliefs and ways to improve upon them.
- How can you develop positive beliefs for managing your feelings better?

Self-Empowering Beliefs

Finally, let us sum up by segregating these beliefs about ourselves into two categories-unhelpful and helpful beliefs. Apart from these given below here you may like to add some of your own ones in the left hand columns and then convert them into realistic ones in the right hand column.

Unhelpful beliefs	*Helpful beliefs*
Emotions are mostly a hindrance to achieving Career growth.	Emotions can also be powerful source of inspiration if properly guided.
I can't control how I feel; my emotions just happen to me.	Most of my emotions have been learned from experience.
We must be competent and perfect	We may make mistake sometimes and learn from it.
I ought to feel upset when things go wrong	I can choose how I feel, even when things go wrong
Events in the external world make me feel angry, worried, guilty, and helpless	I am responsible for deciding how I feel
I am bound to worry about dangerous things that might happen	There is no need to worry; however I may remain alert and take necessary precautions
Things should move in exactly the way I want.	I prefer when things proceed in the way I want them to.
My choices are restricted due to early decisions in my career	My experience and skills can be reinterpreted to fit into emerging areas of growth.

(Contd.)

(Contd. Table)

Unhelpful beliefs	*Helpful beliefs*
It is not possible to practice truly, what I value in life	It may be difficult in one go, but it is possible to get closer to what I consider of value by systematic efforts
It is natural that my day-to-day priorities will take precedence on what I consider personally meaning full in life.	It is always possible to negotiate an arrangement where I am able to do things which are personally meaningful alongside other routine elements
Anxiety about performance or achieving something is detrimental to my growth.	Some amount of anxiety is good and aids in performing well, however too much anxiety can be detrimental to my growth.

Dynamics of beliefs

If your scores are less you may examine how some of the above mentioned unrealistic, beliefs (on the left hand column above) are the cause of it. You may then like to think of ways to replace these unrealistic beliefs with the ones shown in the right-handed column above.

Imagine that you are like a powerful computer but without anti virus installed and therefore you are prone to all sorts of corrupted software, which is impeding your progress and might eventually lead to total system failure. Why to wait till that point and why not install this powerful antivirus now and be vigilant that these positive Beliefs and attitudes (the antivirus) will not allow your thinking process to be corrupted by the various influences in the world.

The thoughts that come to our minds are likes seeds which when allowed taking roots and nurture leads to its own fruits of opportunities and circumstances. Practicing helpful beliefs and good

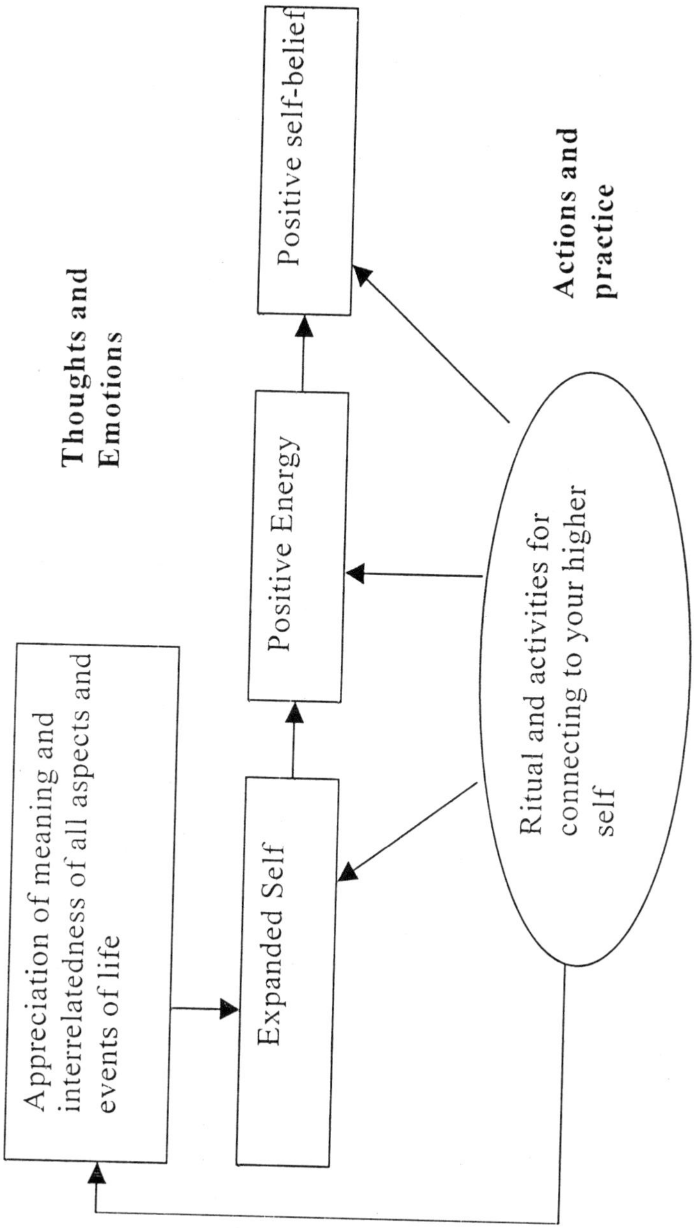

Fig 2.3. The Expended Self.

thoughts leads to bear good fruits. The basis of personal development and career growth are beliefs. Beliefs are positive declarations that guide us and control our reactions to myriads situations of life. Beliefs have a deeper permanent meaning and can direct and change the course of your career and bring lasting happiness in your life.

Many studies have pointed out that the people who are resilient and are able to bounce back from terrible situations in lives are people who have a fundamental belief that there is meaning to every event that happens in their life. It is this fundamental belief which is the genesis for a disposition of being optimistic under all circumstances. By talking to several people who have a very high sense of optimism and resilience in life, I have made a simple model to depict this dynamics of acquiring fundamentally helpful beliefs in life, which is shown in fig 2.3.

To use Self-beliefs in tapping the power of the conscious and subconscious mind, we need to:

Appreciate that there is meaning in every event or situation that is coming to us no matter what it is? Sometimes this meaning may not be apparent to us immediately but if we are patient, the purpose of it will be revealed to us and it would help and guide us at each stage of our life and career.

We can create our own beliefs about self and our unique strengths. This should also include our vision for a fruitful career and rewarding life. Beliefs residing in both conscious and subconscious mind can be strengthened by discovering certain rituals and activities that enrich us and help us in connecting with our higher self. Normally people think of rituals as some religious rites or customary observance in specific times of life cycle like birth, marriage, death etc. Such rituals have definitely a very soothing and positive effect on transition times of our life and help us in generating a positive belief about self and the situation, but I am using the term rituals to include many more of our "personal triggering mechanisms" that helps in putting self in better mental state. So here is a brief definition of what I mean by the term ritual in the context of this chapter.

> Rituals are series of steps for generating "mental patterns" that helps us in drawing out best of our internal resources in terms of positive energies of thoughts, feelings and emotions from within us. In fact, Rituals are the means of repeating and affirming your positive beliefs and making a habit of thinking positive under all circumstances of life.

Let me illustrate by giving an example from what a participant in a seminar told me. "You know when I was a child I was extremely fond of reading "chandamama" –a monthly Hindi magazine with small stories for children. To this date when I have crossed 40, this is the best way to induce the best of my mental patterns. I have subscribed to this magazine and read it before going to bed and it not only helps in inducing a very refreshing and energizing sleep but somehow invokes the best of thoughts and emotions lying dormant from childhood memory."

A sportsman once told me that whenever he wish to enter a higher state, he thinks of the last time when he experienced joy and ecstasy in playing his favorite sport. He regularly uses this feeling to tap into the best of his internal resources and that way gets into the state of positive energy.

Mountaineers who often say that mountains have a magical influence on them share similar experiences and they go for mountaineering or rock climbing to relive those great feelings they get.

When practicing a ritual or repeating a belief, seek total relaxation of body and mind. Then place the affirmation in your mind and hold it there.

Having understood the dynamics of belief and its importance for our growth and development, let us now apply the concept of self-belief to develop a small ritual through the exercise given below, which will help us to discover the positive value in our perceived limitations.

Exercise: Talents and Limitations

To discover positive value inherent in an apparently negative limitations

Many of us give up easily on aspects which we value just because we are stuck by imaginary or perceived limitations. Life of great personalities such as Helen Keller, Stephen Hawkins etc teach us that even severe limitation, can not be an obstacle in our path and in fact we can turn these limitations to sources of great inspiration for meaningful career and life.

So here is an exercise for helping you discover the positive value in an apparent limitation. Always do this exercise along with a person whom you trust such as Spouse, friend or colleague who holds you in high esteem. Take about 15-20 minutes to fill the left hand side of the table given below.

Sl.No	*My Talents*	*My Limitation*

Searching for Positive Value in the limitations

In this exercise, you will work to examine a perceived shortcoming or limitation, which erodes your self-confidence and hinders you in your career growth. You will be using this experience for building self-empowerment in possible future situations. Please follow the instructions carefully and follow the steps, which are briefly described below. After you have completed the exercise, use a Seperate Work Sheet to record your observations.

1. **Examine perceived shortcoming**: Think back of a specific situation when you were aware of or someone pointed to you some limitations/shortcomings of yours. This could be any such thing like a handicap or monetary situation etc.

2. **Appreciate and extract the positive value:** Examine what could be the positive value of this limitation or under what circumstances this limitation would be a positive value etc? Create a self belief that this limitation also has a purpose for your life.

3. **What could be the purpose of this limitation for my career:** Enter into an inner dialogue with yourself and search for alternate ways to extract the positive value from this limitation. Write down all possible alternatives in a piece of paper. Ask a creative part within you or take the help of a partner to assist you to generate lots and lots of possible behaviors that will help you in converting the limitation to something useful for your career.

Sl.No	*My Limitation*	*Positive value in it*

Review and Action Planning

Work out an action plan and discuss with your partner and generate new choices for your career growth.

____

____

____

Personal Action Points arising from the exercise

____

____

____

Here is an inspiring line from Helen Keller, a role model for any one who wishes to search for positive value in his or her limitations.

- **I can see, and that is why I can be happy, in what you call the dark, but which to me is golden. I can see a God- made world, not a manmade world.**
- **Character cannot be developed in ease and quiet. Only through experiences of trial and suffering can the soul be strengthened, vision cleared, ambition inspired and success achieved.**

Helen Keller

The mental model and the challenge ahead

We started this chapter talking about choices that we create for ourselves. Most people think of choices as something that have to be taken from the external environment; however, our most important choices are about how we have chosen to perceive, believe, feel and respond to different situations. The process begins with self awareness and introspection and helps in creating a mental model which generates positive emotions, quality choices and positive outcomes for career growth and joy at work.

Let us remind ourselves that all of us have three basic choices, which largely depend on us.

- The Choice of positive belief- This is the most fundamental choice that have a direct bearing on all other choices.

- Choice of positive associations- This involves associating ourselves with positive thinking, feelings and being with people who are inspiring in their thoughts and actions.

- Choice of positive action- This choice is largely dependent on the first two choices. Our actions derive new meaning and energy, when carried out in combination with the first two choices.

The choices in the external world are often the results of our internal choices. The exercises in this chapter will help you in generating positive mental models and thinking patterns about your self, which is fundamental to empowering one self before further committing to the exciting journey on career growth. The rest of this book is all about generating choices for positive action for career growth and joy at work. So, now brace up for an exciting and challenging journey ahead!

3

Nurturing and Stimulating the Inner Core

Experiencing joy at Work

Stories of great achievers from all walks of life indicate a strong tendency to be completely engrossed in their work. It is somewhat like work becoming as interesting as play or hobby for them. Biographies of as diverse personalities as Albert Einstein, Mahatma Gandhi, Jack Welch, Bill Gates reveals this common thread in their lives. This passion for their chosen field of work or interest is also instrumental in bringing out the best while also experiencing joy at work.

What distinguishes work from play is the satisfaction derived from simply engaging in the activity. An activity which is work for some one can also be play for someone else. For example work out or aerobics can be an activity for someone, making an attempt to slim down. However if the person starts enjoying a feeling of wholeness by loosing self-consciousness in the rhythmic motion, the same activity of jogging becomes play.

Many of us are so conscious of distinction between work and play as a result of our upbringing that it seems almost impossible to bridge the divide. The culture in our work places and the society at large tend to promote this divide between work and play. However, there are some organizations which have promoted this culture of "fun at work". World famous pike fish centre is one such organizations in America, which claims that there employees come to play and not work. A movie has been made about this company and its work philosophy. The movie shows their work culture, the playful activities while working, and involvement of customers in these playful activities etc. An employee in this movie is shown saying-that though they work for 12 hours sometimes, yet they arrive home smiling and relaxed. For these employees those 12 hours are not merely work but also jokes, fun, laughter, good exercise and healthy nutrition that makes them completely rejuvenated even after spending long hours at work. Contrast this with those who return home from office-tired, irritated and exhausted, so much so that some of us need a couple of hours just to set the mood right!

We will be able to enjoy a far more creative, stress free, healthy and productive life if there is fusion of work and play in our daily life. An often comment such as "making a vocation out of my hobby takes the fun out of it" is indicative of this divide between work and play. The roots of which goes to our child hood experiences of play being something totally different than work. The degree of fusion of work and play to a great extent is due to an individual's development history right through his childhood. Introducing play full ness into work activities from child hood would enable the child to respond to the expectations from others in a spontaneous way without feeling a compulsion to do so. This can be done by involving the child in interesting projects that combine certain degree of playful ness with ownership and responsibility to complete the tasks as per the expectations of authority figures. A similar effect is also possible in adults, which can enable us to transform aspects of work in such a way that work itself becomes a source of enjoyment and nourishment for us. We shall examine this through an exercise designed to work out such generic projects that will help you divide this gap for yourself – A concept that we will be returning to later in this chapter.

Most vocational counsellors are familiar with the stereotyped comment "I am looking for something that will give me (good money, security, future prospects etc), for better living and something I will be happy doing. Even when a person struggles with the necessity of finding a livelihood, he or she also tries to seek a personal meaning and some form of creative expression. Most individuals have a secret desire to participate in their career with their complete personality. For many people, this desire remains unarticulated or subconscious. However the individual's wish for a wholesome organized life operates in a silent manner as his inner guidance mechanism.

This silent and unseen guidance mechanism steers them through the course of selecting a training course, job entry and job change decisions etc., ever seeking to increase the congruence between intrinsic satisfaction that work provides and personal orientation and needs. It may be possible to infer this enduring orientation from understanding significant patterns of individual's life history especially by examining feelings, fantasies, dreams, and other imaginative responses directed to past, present or future. We shall be going through this process through an exercise later in this chapter.

Developing an Ideal Fit between Self and Work

It is the fit that transforms the imperative to work (in order to survive) into a meaningful vocation. This fit is the means through which necessity is converted into self–fulfilment. In the words of Gardener "What can be more satisfying than to be engaged in a work in which every capacity or talent one may have is needed, every lesson one may have learned is used, every value one care about is furthered."

We are looking for that "super string" where we can put all the beads together, for developing this ideal fit between self and work. Our endeavour is to search for the common thread, which would give a meaning to every aspect of our life including career or work. This process of getting into an ideal fit between self and work is not a mechanistic process but more like an evolutionary process which needs patience and constant self introspection. Since the occupations and person evolve over a period of time, the steering process of seeking an ideal fit involves the changing factors of self and the occupation. The younger the person the more it is possible to change the personality to suit the requirements of the work or career. In some ways we are moulded by the work situations or challenges we face, at the same time we also mould the situations at work to suit our requirements.

A subconscious process guides us through a string of decisions, which take us to different types of work or jobs. This mechanism influences the cognitive process through which we as individuals assess alternatives at each point. This choice may arise from external structure, for example the next stage in the education process or next step in professional progress or job movement. It may also arise from internal structure i.e. feeling of deprivation or positive feeling of enlarging ones satisfaction etc. It is essentially a process of finding a good fit between our inner calling and external opportunities-a process that we will talk about when we go into the depth of the concept of Generic project and its application in our real life situation.

Whether the Daily Work Nurtures Your Inner Core

There are times when we are fully energized, full of ideas, curiosity, looking forward to the day as it unfolds events and situations. The very alertness and positive energy makes us vibe well with our surroundings and help us in getting the best out of the possibilities that emerge. There are also times when we are depressed, down under, unsure of ourselves and full of negative thoughts, where life seems to be full of drudgery and nothing seem to work in our favor. The most fortunate people are those, in whose life the first one is the default setting and no matter what happens they keep bouncing back to the highly optimistic state. We call such people resilient-those who are able to bounce back from any situation, problem or setback.

Have you ever wondered how do they bounce back ,when they go down under the currents-what is that life guard that help them to bounce back to surface and then resume their journey forward. In most cases you will see that this life guard is nothing but a project about which they are passionate and hence that helps them to find meaning in life even after a setback.

So we need to discover such a Generic Project, for nourishing and strengthening of self on daily basis. Whether you do have a Generic Project –Stated or unstated, about which you are conscious or not, you need to have a project that nurtures that inner core of yours. Most importantly you need to see whether your daily work helps in nurturing that core or it only makes it whither away. Does the daily grind helps in sharpening the axe? Or makes it blunt making your work even more difficult.

So here is a questionnaire, a sort of check list-which tells you whether your work, the daily grind is aligned to your "inner core".

1. I actively plan to create "some time" for activities of my choice during working hours.

2. I weave in elements which are of personal interest to me while planning my job/work.

3. There is always a curiosity while getting to work as to what might happen.

4. I always look forward to meeting some people and seeking new ideas from them while in my work.

5. There are aspects in my work which stimulate my thinking and I look forward to return to them when the routine work is over.

6. The work place gives me an opportunity to acquire important information about my profession or field of inertest.

7. My work also provides an opportunity to interact with inspiring people.

8. I find harmony, beauty and colors in my work environment.

9. While in my work environment, I often feel I am being trained for aspects which are personally very important in my life.

10. My work environment helps me in bringing out my talents.

11. There are interesting coincidences at work, which turn out to be useful later.

12. The work and its related aspects contribute to my mental and physical health.

If the answers of many the above questions is NO, Chances are that you are doing a job which does not stimulates and nurture your "Core". However that does not necessarily mean that the type of Job you are in right now is completely unsuitable for you. It may just be that you are not interpreting your job in the right manner. You will be surprised to know that in many cases it is possible to redesign or add some new elements in your job by your own initiative which would make your job very interesting to you.

In fact to do that you must first understand your inner core in terms of your unique strengths and resources. Many a time this awareness can help you to realize that your job can possibly have elements or activities which are personally very important to you.

Perplexity in Career Decisions Points are due to Doubts about the Self

Events, experiences and influences all through developmental stages of an individual can have an influence on later career. It is therefore important to look beyond the formal experiences of the school and college and also examine other personal aspects, which have a role to play in our growth and development. Normal development of any individual is not a smooth and continuous process. In the process of development, the individual derives the strengths and weaknesses of those he is close to. He also seeks to overcome those weaknesses to build an independent existence of his.

Some time accumulated dissatisfactions and doubts are likely to culminate in particular decision point. These decision points may be due to the norms and expectations set up by the educational system or world of work, special conditions created by slump or technological development or some personal tragedy for the individual. Because these situations represent pressure to re-examine personal resolutions, they also represent opportunities to rework those resolution in the direction of fuller self-realization and satisfaction. Resolving and clarifying self and building a longer term perspective on what constitutes source of satisfaction and growth for individual is of utmost important for individual in his quest for evaluating decision at transition points.

Change is eternal. And the fittest ones who survive are those who adapt the fastest to change. However, the challenging task is to identify what are the changes that one needs to adapt to? In this task, the essential requirement is how to draw a fine demarcation between the strategic determinants for career growth and the "inner core" in terms of unique strengths and values or work ideology of an individual. The "inner core" of an individual is a time tested component that needs to be nurtured and preserved while the specific manifestation of that core must be open for evaluation and change .The concept, which is now described, helps precisely in this process. The exercise, which follows the concept, is particularly useful at the transition times.

Generic Project(s) as Your Long Term Ally

I do not know whether you have observed in your life, the most important source of happiness is your work. In our life we have to do several things which can be classified as work. Things like meeting customers, attending to their complaints, worrying about how to make fruitful investment of our savings and how to ensure quality education for our children.

When each of these tasks remains an independent piece of work with no connection with each other, life appears to be short for all your aspirations and goals. However when there is a possibility of a synthesis on several such important aspects of work and career, life becomes a harmonious whole. It becomes possible to do justice to several areas of responsibility with some degree of satisfaction. It is somewhat like that with progress on each aspect of your life, you also seem to contribute to the progress to that which is of critical importance in life. That is the point of generic Project. It is aimed at providing a unifying principle to the different aspects of your work and career, thereby enabling you to get the most from your life.

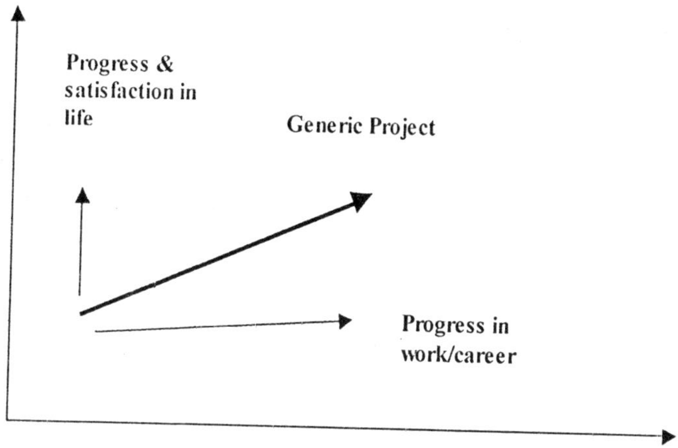

Fig 3.1. Generic Project : The Unifying Principle

The closest thing that comes to my mind to describe this term generic Project (GP) is borrowed from the world of medicine. Have you heard of generic drug in the context of medicine? The generic drug is the basic chemical composition, which helps the pharmacist offer you the choice of the alternative drugs when he does not have the exact drug that your doctor has prescribed. Sometime the generic drug is as effective as the one prescribed by the doctor and also cheaper one. So if you know the generic drug, you have more choices available depending on your budget etc., provided you have reliable information regarding the quality of these various choices available to you.

Generic project works in a similar manner in the field of work and career growth. It is an instrument, which gives you the flexibility to choose from the various opportunities that are available to you without depending on any particular prescribed or normative one. Generic project is your vehicle to develop competencies in a broad area of your interest, which is of great importance from long-term point of view. The generic project is also a sort of method for aligning your self, your goals –professional/personal and other day to day activities, etc in such a way so that it can be instrumental for achieving your dreams as envisaged in the best scenarios which you could draw about yourself for future.

Generic projects are designed to chance upon or expand the use of our special aptitude, resources, talents, specific advantages, information, contacts etc that can support our present or future profession, career, etc. Generic project is both guided by certain constraints or circumstances and the type of opportunities due to our inherent strength. The formal definition of Generic Project provided in chapter I, is repeated here for ease of reference.

Generic Project (GP): The long term project which you constantly look forward to returning and which gives you a constant purpose and focus and which is not necessarily depended on a particular desk or a position you occupy but is rather something more enduring – something which arises out of the inner calling but gets a concrete shape after mulling over the world of external opportunities and the cues that they provide to you.

Here is a short anecdote that demonstrates how generic project works for developing a better fit between career and self.

Developing a better fit between self and Career: A short anecdote

Ravi was never sure whether he wanted this job or not? At the time there seemed to be no other option. Well, Ravi had completed his graduation-barely managing to pass; so there was no possibility of getting an admission in any worthwhile PG course.

Most people will describe Ravi as an introvert, who does not easily make friends and is also not very assertive, when it comes to interactions with others. He was bit lean, thin and of weak physical constitution. Though he knew that the job is not really suitable to him given his temperament and personality, still he took it because there appeared to be no choice at the time.

Apart from this Ravi's friend Krishnan who was doing relatively well in this job convinced him that working with this company, crystal corporation as sales cum commission agent is not a bad idea at all and that Ravi can make a decent living out of it if he puts in 6-8 hrs of good work every day. Besides this it would also give him the experience to apply for better jobs, once he got the desired experience.

From the very beginning Ravi found the job a total nightmare for him. He found the task of meeting different people very arduous. He was no where near the targets and what ever clients he could get, was due to the lead provided by his friend. Boss was not at all happy with him and reprimanded him several times. Out of total sales force of 42, his achievement in terms of overall figures for the first quarter was 3rd from the bottom. Even that was due to the fact that out of the last 2, one was on sick leave and another guy had already made up his mind to leave and would eventually put his papers in due course. Under this scenario Ravi could survive for one full year, because he had this quality of unquestioning loyalty to the boss and ever eagerness to help him in any sort of work he was asked to do.

It was about this time, that Ravi met with a minor accident while driving on his way to a prospective client. It was not something very serious but only a minor dislocation of his right arm. This accident came as a blessing in disguise, for it put him out of active field job for the next 2 months. It was during this period that Ravi was assigned some desk job involving keeping track of payments, ensuring MIS to the head office. Ravi excelled in this job.

This two months job brought out following aspects of Ravi's abilities and traits which were appreciated both by his boss and other colleagues.

1. Being methodical and systematic in paper work.

2. Patient and tactful in following up with defaulting customers.

3. Humility and eagerness to help in any sort of work.

These strengths of Ravi points to his generic project: Gaining an edge through respecting seniors, helping nature and systematic work. This ability when nurtured would eventually help him in getting a break in accordance to his nature. Due to his unquestioning loyalty to his former boss, Ravi could get a recommendation as front desk manger in a Show room of well known brand in clothing. Gradually Ravi learnt professional aspects of his new job. His penchant for being systematic coupled with patience in handling customer provided a reasonably good career for him.

This story demonstrates that often the seeds of our career growth are around us and we only need to discover and nurture them to realize their full potential. In this story you saw that Ravi's inherent strength pertaining to work and career got discovered as a result of chance. Similarly many of our unique strengths are revealed under special circumstances. Such strengths points to – what should be our Generic project, a project which would eventually provide us a unique edge and opportunity in our career and life.

Understanding Significant Patterns and Strengths of Your Life

Think back of some key events or beginnings in your life. How did it happen? You will find life full of such coincidences like this. You bumped into an old friend that you hadn't met for some time and he told you about the job in his company. You learnt swimming because of the convenient location of pool near your office and because you wanted an ongoing excuse for avoiding sitting late at office. You got an article published because of a new acquaintance giving you a valuable contact reference. The lesson in all such experiences is that when we are ready to make a new beginning, we find an opportunity. But we can make much more of these experiences if we take a genuine interest in our self and be alert and open to the opportunities around us.

The true secret of happiness lies in taking a genuine interest in all details of your daily life and elevating them to an art.

-William Morris

So let us take a cue from this and begin a process to discover our generic project through an exercise designed for this purpose.

Exercise: Understanding Significant Patterns and Strengths of Your Life

This exercise is aimed at helping you to understand those significant patterns in you life that has an overall positive intention for your growth and development. While doing this exercise consider your entire life from childhood till now and consider each items marked A to E, in chronological order to choose 3-5 incidents under each category and then describe as per table given below. While describing the situation, consider each event as a positive and important incident, in which there is a hidden meaning for you. You are now in a journey to unearth this meaning for unlocking the secrets of success, which are unique for you through this exercise. While doing this exercise think of yourself like a detective, trying to decipher the significant patterns of your life as if you are working to unfold the secret of a great story which is still in the process of becoming.

Step 1

In the first step record the significant patterns and their positive intentions for your career as per the format given below.

A. Significant Achievements for which you were praised or recognized

Sl.No.	*Year*	*Brief Description*	*Positive Intentions*

B. Significant Expectations from you (by yourself /your heroes/ teachers etc.)

Sl.No.	Year	Brief Description	Positive Intentions

C. Significant Influences (by people/books/ideas etc.)

Sl.No.	Year	Brief Description	Positive Intentions

D. Significant Experiences (of learning, ispiration, insight etc.)

Sl.No.	Year	Brief Description	Positive Intentions

E. Significant advantages (Qualifications, critical resources, information, contacts, friends etc.)

Sl.No.	Year	Brief Description	Positive Intentions

F. Significant personal strengths (Values, aptitude, skill, habit, talent, health etc.)

Sl.No.	*Year*	*Brief Description*	*Positive Intentions*

Step 2

In this step you may play with the data generated about various patterns in your life by first codifying all the significant patterns you have recorded above as a unique code such as A1, B2, C3, F5 etc and then mixing/merging/combining/modifying/eliminating as you may like. While doing this assume that all the strengths of these significant patterns are available to you at present irrespective of the fact that many of these may have been in the past.

1. Now use the format below to combine these pattern in various ways and describe what type of new insights are emerging as to the new possibilities in your life. you may also put it from the perspective of what might have happened if every thing must have come about in best possible ways by combining these patterns of your life. While writing describe what you could be achieving through your own

Sl. No.	*A*	*B*	*C*	*D*	*E*	*F*	*Scenario (Future possibilities)*
I	1	1	1	1	1	1	
II	1	2	2	3	3	2	
III							

strengths and resources (as you have worked out in step 1) in the right hand column of the table given below.

2. Write at least three possible future scenarios based on above exercise.

Developing your Generic Project

In this step you will be working out your generic project. Generic project is your vehicle to develop the competencies in a broad area of your interest, which is of great importance from long-term point of view. The generic project is also a sort of method for aligning your self, your goals –professional/personal and other day to day activities, etc. in such a way so that it can be instrumental for achieving your dreams as envisaged in the best scenarios which you could draw about yourself in future.

While designing your generic project do remember the following salient features of a generic project before you proceed further.

Features of the Generic Project

1. It helps in developing a broad range of capabilities.

2. It should be in line with your aptitude or special interest

3. It should not be narrowly defined, so that you can maintain your flexibility to benefit from new opportunities.

4. It should not be only of academic interest but it may be such that it could also be of economic significance for you or someone close to you /friends/family members etc.

Based on the above features, define your generic project(s) with a view to increase your general understanding of emerging opportunities in certain broad area as well as developing your competence in that area. Some examples of generic project are as given below. You may make your own examples corresponding to the future scenarios worked out by you in step 2 of the above exercise. Some examples of Generic Projects are given below:

Developing unique strength and gaining an edge by.....

- Absorbing knowledge of concepts and techniques in a field of interest with purpose of selection in competitive exams

- Sourcing, coordinating and integrating the outputs of several individual to meet the organizational goals.

- Being innovative, flexible and responsive to markets and opportunities with entrepreneurial bent of mind

- Authoring of new ideas and inventions, patenting and copywriting of these

- Technical expertise in a specialized field, usually with a professional degree, license etc

- Contribution of emotional or aesthetic appeal due to a talent or work of art etc

- Imparting knowledge and skills, facilitating learning in groups or classes

- Developing qualities like empathy, patience and willingness to help others

- Networking, public relations and Liaisoning work, benefiting through contacts, references testimonials etc.

- Disciplined and hardworking, efficient in executing what is told in precise manner

- Strong Logic and objective reasoning

- Knack for using and maintaining machines
- Accuracy and speed in calculations
- Flair for learning languages and other cultures and traditions
- Flair for physical activities, outdoor and adventurous life style
- Acute sense of observation, systematic investigation to deduce meaning from information
- Preferring a flexible working thru home based services to allow integration of personal and professional concerns.

These are some generic projects which would be applicable to people, however this is not certainly an exhaustive list and you may formulate something which is customized to your specific needs. From the above list or on your own you may choose upto 3 generic projects which are going to be useful to you both from the perspective of career growth as well as joy at work. It may also be possible to combine different aspects of the Generic projects chosen by you to form another GP that suits your requirement better.

Take into Account Your Current Reality while Planning Your GP

The normal approach of many self-help books is to give you big dreams, which are totally away from your current reality, which often leads to creating threatening situations in your current job or responsibilities etc. While designing your generic project it is extremely important to pay attention to various details regarding how you will find time from your current occupation so that you can work it out at least some part of it in your day to day activities. So test your generic project feasibility from the perspective of current reality.

For many people important transitions in life and career are always accompanied by some hints or clues in the form of an "idea" or "impression" or "image". It is difficult to describe this, but it involves imagining some scene or activity and feeling attracted to it. You may be already doing it at times without realizing it. It is something like a half formed dream, which you are hardly conscious. The process of working out the GP helps you in bringing this vision into consciousness and thus facilitating this process of inner realignment and constant renewal of energy. It is like having a definite strategy for chance to work in your favor. So now describe your GP in your own words and write it down for future reference.

Developing Your GP: An Illustrative Example

To help the readers understand the process better, here is an example of a university professor developing his Generic project around his unique strengths and circumstances. Since professors are usually good at conceptualizing, you can see in this example how the professor has used this exercise to synthesize aspects of work and life into an interesting Generic project suitable to his needs, values and aptitude. After going through the steps in the exercise given in this chapter, the professor selected the following 03 generic projects from the ready made list provided in this Chapter.

1. Authoring of new ideas, inventions and creation. Patenting and Copywriting of these.

2. Technical expertise in a specialized field with little distraction of administrative or managerial work.

3. Being innovative, flexible and responsive to new opportunities with entrepreneurial bent of mind.

Out of the above list the first 2 are very close to professor's heart as these are in accordance to his Values, needs and special aptitude. However the third one though not as close to his heart as the first 2, has also been considered because of the current reality of the professor's situation. Since the availability of university grant for carrying out research is declining and there is more emphasis on generating own resources through consultancy assignments for supplementing the research activities, therefore the professor has also considered the 3rd one as a possible candidate for generic project in line with his requirement.

Apart from this, the third GP also opens up the possibility of profit sharing as a result of revenue earning through the consulting assignments. Since the 3rd GP is a new area for the professor, the professor works out a strategic alliance with the placement in-charge, who has excellent PR and liaison skills, so as to be able to get the required help for gaining an edge in his work and career.

Based on this exercise the professor finally combines the relevant elements of the above Generic projects to work out his unique GP that is likely to sustain his career interest and enthusiasm for long term success. This is as described below.

- **Excellence through applied research, its publications and patenting. Increasing applications for industry thru consultancy work in collaboration with other supportive agencies and departments.**

Taking a cue form the professor's example try to work out generic projects which you think will be supportive for your career growth and long term success. Think of people whom you need to consult to further refine your generic project. You may take the help of your friends or colleagues for this. Your generic project has to be something that would be valid and applicable for you at least for a period of 3 years and must help you build your competencies in broad area of work, so you need to think about this carefully and take some time. It is no point only keeping this in mind, so do make an attempt to describe your generic project in the space provided using a pencil. This if for your reference and use in the next and subsequent chapters; where we have more applications of this subject.

Brief description of your GP

____

____

____

In this chapter we have just made a beginning for developing our Generic project around our natural strengths and circumstances. In the next chapter we will examine way and means to further refine the generic project and get the best opportunities for our career growth and long term success.

4

Opening New Avenues with Your GP

Have you ever wondered why you feel so scholarly when you sit in a well-organized library? The very ambience of the library-the quite atmosphere, availability of various books and the organized look makes you feel good about reading there. Have you ever walked into an appealing restaurant, where there is the sight and aroma of delicious food, along with the right ambience and courteous staff? The whole experience makes you hungrier for your favorite food. The same is true for your GP, the more appealing a configuration you give it, the hungrier and motivated you become to achieve the results of your GP.

Building an appropriate configuration is similar to this ambience described above. It is something like creating a motivating environment around you, which is so energizing that the entire process of making an effort becomes a worthwhile experience. So you do not merely look forward to the end results but also learn to enjoy the process. This of course doesn't mean that the results are not important. They are important and we will talk about it shortly, however it is more important for you to enjoy this process of growth and development during your journey of GP because ultimately it is the area of your interest and you have yourself committed to it.

To give you an analogy, if you are passionate about some sports like soccer, what would be the fun if you were only interested in winning every game? On the contrary if you become too conscious of winning all the time, you will not be able to concentrate on your natural game and eventually that will disturb your co-ordination. The same is true for any worthwhile endeavour in life about which you ought to be passionate, because if you are not passionate, you will not be able to bring the energy that is demanded for success in life.

Building this ambience calls for setting up what I call a configuration suitable for carrying out the GP. Configuration is something like an arrangement surrounding your life or your day-to day activities. This is something similar to what we described about a well-organized library or an appealing restaurant, which makes you hungrier- the first one for knowledge and the latter for food. For ease of understanding and implementation, we can divide this into 2 categories as follows.

1. Maintenance Configuration
2. Achievement configuration

Maintenance Configuration

Maintenance configuration is that arrangement which enables a person to reduce the disorderliness that will come due to being increasingly busy pursuing specific targets pertaining to a focused area of interest. There is an interesting law of physics which says that the total amount of entropy (read disorderliness) of a system increases with the passage of time. Something similar also happens to human beings. As we make more progress in respect of our GP, we become more orderly there, but then disorderliness sets in somewhere else in our personal life etc. You may say that this is true for physical substances and that I may be exaggerating it's effect one humans. So, let me give you some concrete pieces of evidence from the lives of great people, who experienced great entropy in their personal lives about the time when their professional career was at peak.

Take the case of the greatest scientist of the 20th century - Albert Einstein. It was just about the time, when he came up with his master piece –special theory of relativity that his personal life was in shambles, his relationship with his wife was at its lowest. Another case in point is Michael Faraday, brilliant scientist and the discoverer of electricity. At the time of his most astounding discoveries, he was a bachelor. So his problems couldn't have been from the spouse, but from his erstwhile mentor-Sir Davie, who being envious of his mentee's success, was bent upon creating hurdles upon hurdles in his path. Haven't you seen similar things happening to you? Just recall the time when you were doing very well in your focused area of interest, when something went wrong somewhere else Personal or professional.

There are some functions in our daily life that enable us to be normal, healthy and free of worry so that we can take the more important challenges of life with enough attention and time. We need to carry out many such maintenance functions so that daily irritants do not bog us down. Mundane routine aspects like ensuring regular payment of bills, ensuring a healthy diet, filing important papers, daily exercise, getting a haircut, filing income tax return etc.

These small things can take away a lot of our time and will cause distraction when we are busy with important work connected to our GP. A software professional while developing software for an important client, commented thus- "the more time I need for this project and the closer I am to solving the main problem, the more I am distracted by both problems at home as well as Office". When asked how it is so, he said "I need to work with a guy who has come from abroad and is going back in a day or two, and now you see my daughter is ill, boss has given me some donkeywork to be completed in 2 days. "It is impossible to mange the two". It all sounds familiar-isn't it, something similar to the good old Murphy's Law!

Common, lets face it children will be falling ill once in a while, boss will give an important deadline at the wrong time and relatives will land at your house precisely at the time when you don't want them there. So how do we deal with this? Our common sense approach to deal with these challenges is by negotiating these issues as and when they come, taking help from friends and may be spouse to deal with them one at a time. While negotiation is fine for those sudden developments that we can't plan, but there are certain things which could be put in place with an effective maintenance configuration.

The first aspect of your maintenance configuration is how much time and energy efficient it is. How efficiently the maintenance activities can be carried out so that you get more time and energy left to pursue your dream projects. The first thing to do is to thus give up many activities, which are not of direct use to your GP. Remember- Bill gates and how he told his mother that he would not be able to speak to any one for the next six months because of an important project.

Ask Yourself these key questions?

- What do I do so that I do not have to do this activity for the next six months? Or never at all?
- What do I do so that it would take a very small amount of time per week at a time, and when I am free to do this?

- What do I do, so that I can combine certain routine activities and take care of them at the same time?

- What can I do to delegate this routine activity to a person who has to do this activity anyway periodically?

Having Started with all Negatives, now Consider some Positive Ones-

- How can I ensure sufficient healthy nutrition, so that I remain energetic the whole day?

- How can I ensure some form of good exercise so that I remain energetic the whole day?

- How can I ensure sufficient sleep and rest, so that I remain energetic the whole day?

Principle of Destroying Entropy by Combining two Negatives

A few years back, I observed a boss of mine who was very fond of eating away all my time by engaging in endless and fruitless discussion in the garb of official and important discussion. After endless thought on how to save my time, I came up with a novel solution. Upon close examination I found another guy who was equally talkative and loved this wonderful art of endless discussion. So all I did is bring along this guy saying it will be interesting to listen to his views as well. Then I simply vanished at the opportune time, and collected the important information of the decision or lack of it that came as a result of their discussion.

Principle of Destroying Entropy by Proactively Deciding what You Want To Do

In one of my seminars a participant asked me - what is a good way to avoid the "donkey work" that boss keeps assigning. I replied -tell me to whom such work gets assigned in general to any one in home. I asked him to think about his own family and tell how such "thank less" jobs are assigned, and he then murmured

– Such jobs are assigned to the one who is free and who is doing nothing. He volunteered that most things get assigned to his son after he is found wasting time, loitering here and there and talking on phone. That's it -You can only avoid unnecessary work by volunteering to to do important activities on your own in a proactive manner.

Making the Most of Necessary Evil

When you are unable to avoid "thankless" work, think that even this has relevance for your generic project. Who knows- there may be some hidden meaning for you? A sales man once told me this interesting incident, where he was given the dirty job of collecting payments from a defaulter. He was trying to avoid it for too long, but now found it difficult without exposing the so-called "negative attitude" to the higher ups. He later realized that one of his friends was also located in the building next to this client. This later chance meeting lead to establishing a part time consultancy work in partnership. As far as the payment from that defaulter is concerned it never came and the issue was referred to the legal department, nevertheless a good opportunity was spotted and utilized by having a proactive approach.

I know an insurance agent who planned visits to haircutting saloons in such a way so as to meet prospective clients. He was able to do good business by the chance interactions at haircutting saloons. A man had to spend long hours for commuting everyday in a chartered bus, so he used this time by listening to audio books in areas of his interest. He networked with some fellow passengers and they exchanged their audio books and thus he could go through several interesting books for which he could not find time earlier.

Mechanize Routine Activities

Many of us like to buy the latest gizmos, but how many of us use all the features wisely? Using mobile phones, computer, email, fax and other gazettes for saving time is also an art. The time spent in learning these features, which makes you more productive, will repay you many times in coming years. Set up arrangements with prospective suppliers, service agents, and bankers to give you reminders about when to renew your car insurance, new schemes, servicing of car, free check up etc. One of my neighbors gets a call from a big merchandize store, whenever there is a sale in the store. This way one can save time as well as money also.

Keep Important Documents Safe and Handy

Just recall the pain and agony of a person who is unable to find an important paper at the right time. Then try to imagine the amount of time lost in looking for important papers, the stress it leads to and, the lost opportunity. I am sure you will fully understand the importance of this. Keeping oneself organized is one of the surest ways of avoiding Murphy's Law, jeopardizing your plans and making your life hell. While people do take care of the office related papers and documents, they often tend to forget to take care of their personal papers at home. So make it a practice to file all sorts of paper that are likely to be of use in future such as medical prescriptions, bank statements, IT returns, investment details etc. in separate folders.

A good practice is to buy a large Ring folder with several subsections, marked with colored pages (separators), so that you can easily refer to any paper when you need to. Some people complain that they do get so many documents from diverse sources that they are unable to even figure out what to do with them. When you are not sure whether a particular document is of any importance, do not rush to destroy it in a hurry; instead keep it in a transition file for some time. The transition file should contain any such paper for which you don't have the time and papers that you would like to keep for a short time. Periodically, review the contents of the transition file, when you have more time and then decide which one needs to be weeded out and which one must be placed in the appropriate section of your main file.

Achievement Configuration

Achievement configuration is all about those arrangements in your daily life which help you in effective planning and execution that facilitates your GP. This is about deciding what you want to achieve in the short and long term and how you are going to achieve it. The first step in this is to consider the low hanging fruits. The low hanging fruits, which you know need to keep coming so that you keep getting feedback and reinforcement. Such feedback and motivation is very important for sustaining efforts to achieve your cherished goals.

Low hanging fruits that are facilitative to your GP.

In the hope of achieving big dreams, we must not forget the low hanging fruits that life has to offer. It is the accumulation of these small fruits that make us feel good on an everyday basis and continue to inspire for bigger dreams. In a way it boosts our enthusiasm. First step is identifying some low hanging fruits that are good for keeping your moral high on your GP. There can be many such as getting a good return on your investment, getting your son or daughter into a professional college, being able to buy an expensive gift for your spouse etc. The key point is to first identify them so that you know in advance what will sustain your motivation for the long haul. Some of these may be indirectly supportive to your GP but may work wonder for sustaining your enthusiasm in the long run. Make a list of those that are directly or indirectly affecting your GP.

Low hanging fruits that are poisonous for your GP.

Now think of those low hanging fruits, which though look very attractive, are likely to take you away from your preferred destination. In identifying these low hanging fruits-you need to find out what you definitely want or not. It is something like knowing that there may be some low hanging fruits, which though are very attractive, may be poisonous. It is not only about the proverbial forbidden fruit!

It is important to know what is good for you and what is definitely not considering your GP. Otherwise, you may get drawn to a short term target at the expense of a much more important long term goal. In deciding this, don't treat official, professional or personal targets as separate because the entire idea of GP is to weave the achievements of your dreams into the fabric of your daily life.

Achievement configuration involves not defining targets that are fixed forever but to keep defining new targets as per the emerging opportunities. We have already talked about the visible and important targets in the form of low hanging fruits, where the feedback is immediate. In case of the low hanging fruit, you get the feedback as soon as you take the desired initiative. This feedback can broadly be of 2 types-tangible and intangible. Tangibles involve a formal reward in the form of payment, a sale proceed, a contract being awarded, an incentive earned, advance paid, an honorarium earned or a formal appreciation/recognition letter, membership of a exclusive club. Intangibles may include other types of rewards or recognition, which may lead to credibility as an expert, invitation for soliciting your views, keeping you informed of important developments etc.

Here again you need to know what tangible or intangible rewards you need to seek and what you need to avoid. If you are not very clear on what you need to avoid, a short-term gain at the cost of more important gain may satisfy you. Well, your achievement configuration is all about setting important goals and then finding time and energy to pursue them. Deciding on short term goals is relatively easy because here the feedback is very clear. It is deciding the long-term goals, that there is delayed feedback, and it impacts in the long run.

How do we decide on goals, where the feedback is delayed or is likely to take some time before we come to know whether our decision was right or not? Deciding on these goals is like investing in a property with a hope that its prices will rise in the future. How do we know whether our decision is right or not? Though we can pick up some goals, which are for short term, and long term. Our challenge is to convert longer-term goals into small steps so that we keep getting some feedback at each intermediate step. This keeps your enthusiasm growing and also tells you whether you are in the right direction. Let me illustrate this with an example-A sales man selling beauty products for ladies decided to set up his own shop. First he used his job experience to understand the preferences of his clients-beauty parlors. He soon found that they are interested in products such as Wax of good quality but not necessarily branded ones. So he started supplying his home made wax along with other company products. Checked its feedback, added more products and then eventually went in to set up his business in a systematic step-by-step manner.

Our commitment to the various goals must be in proportion to the positive feedback that we are able to derive from them. However apart from tangible and formal rewards, we also need to take into account the intangible and informal reward that we get such as that of a learning opportunity or networking opportunity etc. What you may ignore as intangible reward may be a new beginning and an upcoming opportunity.

Rating on Twin Perspectives

In the last chapter, there was an exercise for helping you work out your GP.The exercise that now follows will help you in generating more choices from a suggested list of GP. In this exercise you need to rate a possible list of GP's (including the GP you have worked out in last chapter) on the twin aspects of "inner Calling "and "external opportunities".

Inner calling is based on your needs, values, passions and orientation in general. There are some psychological tools that throw light on what can be considered as your inner calling. A list of these psychological tools is provided in the Resource list at the end of this book, which you may find useful. You may also like to supplement your understanding gained thru the exercises in this book (especially in chapter III) by using these psychological tools. External Opportunities is a subjective assessment of the question- what kind of opportunities may emerge for me and my near/dear ones in the long run. Again you may like to supplement your understanding by following the latest developments in your career or field of interest.

After going through this process of introspection and inner dialogue generated through the previous exercises, please rate the GP's shown in the next page on the twin criteria of Inner Calling and External opportunities on a scale of 0-4, with 0-indicating no strong desire or possibility and 4 - indicative of extremely strong inner calling or external opportunity.

You may then work out an over all rating by simply averaging the scores. Alternatively you may also assign weightages, 0: little or no weightage 1: medium 2: High 3: Very high to each of the twin perspectives and then work out the overall rating.

After selecting the generic projects that are important to you, ponder over the following aspects.

- Values or passion perspective (How such a project is important to me personally?)
- Learning or aptitude perspective (What new or definite competencies I need to develop in future if I take up this project?)

Exersice : Ratings on Twin Criterior

Generic Projects *Developing unique strength and gaining an edge by.....*	*Ratings on twin perspectives (High Medium Low)*		*Overall Rating*
	Internal calling	*External Opportunities*	
Absorbing knowledge of concepts and techniques in a field of interest with purpose of selection in competitive exams			
Sourcing, coordinating and integrating the outputs of several individuals to meet the organizational goals.			
Being innovative, flexible and responsive to new opportunities with entrepreneurial mind set.			
Authoring of new ideas and inventions, patenting and copywriting of these			
Technical expertise in a specialized field, usually with a professional degree, license etc.			

(Contd.)

(Contd. Table)

Generic Projects ***Developing unique strength and gaining an edge by.....***	***Ratings on twin perspectives (High Medium Low)***		***Overall Rating***
	Internal calling	***External Opportunities***	
Contribution of emotional or aesthetic appeal due to a talent or work of art etc.			
Imparting knowledge and skills, facilitating learning in groups or classes			
Developing qualities like empathy, patience and willingness to help others			
Networking, public relations and Liaisoning work, benefiting through contacts, references testimonials etc.			
Disciplined and hardworking, efficient in executing what is told in precise manner			
Strong Logic and reasoning skills			
Knack for using and maintaining machines			
Accuracy and speed in calculations			

(Contd.)

(Contd. Table)

Generic Projects ***Developing unique strength and gaining an edge by…..***	***Ratings on twin perspectives (High Medium Low)***		***Overall Rating***
	Internal calling	***External Opportunities***	
Flair for learning languages and other cultures and traditions			
Flair for physical activities, outdoor and adventurous life style			
Acute sense of observation, systematic investigation to deduce meaning from information			
Preferring a flexible working thru home based services to allow integration of personal and professional concerns.			
Custom designed by you at the end of chapter III or Any Other you wish to consider			

- Opportunities or Networking perspective (What kind of opportunities may emerge for me or my near /dear ones? Will it be possible to network with some friends for developing a mutually satisfying opportunity in future?)

- Current Reality Perspective (to what extent a particular generic project is supported by my current occupation, responsibilities etc, this may help in redefining or modifying your GP to suit your current reality more)

Profiling your Generic Project

Having worked out your GP and further refined it, you are now well poised to spell out the various factors that will facilitate your GP. These could be various factors such as - Sources of further information, Types of competencies (skills that you need to develop), Persons with whom you can collaborate, resources or assets, which you may need etc.

In the following exercise, imagine what environment factors and other factors will help you in nurturing or facilitating your GP, using the three step process described below.

1. Imagine what type of ideal state will be needed, so that your generic project moves in a smooth manner? Alternatively, imagine if everything were going right in relation to your generic project then what type of environment you will be having.

Sl.No.	*Environmental factors*	*Choice that will facilitate my GP*	*How Can I get it*
1.	My place of stay		
2.	My place of work		
3.	Book, information source, website etc.		
4.	Any Hobbies or interests etc.		

(Contd.)

(Contd. Table)

Sl.No.	*Environmental factors*	*Choice that will facilitate my GP*	*How Can I get it*
5.	Any Memberships		
6.	Preferred coworker (s)		
7.	Any helpful habits		
8.	Resources like computers, fax, mobile, Internet connection etc		
9.	Skills that may be useful		
10.	Exposure to working in some related area which may be useful		

2. Out of the above list in relation to your generic project, think of those, which can have an overall impact on the enabling environment for doing better in your GP?

(a) Think of people who are already in a better position with respect to each of the resources you have listed above. They may or may not be having the same GP as yours. Now work out possibilities to meet such people and get more information about how to get these resources for you also.

(b) Think of possible areas of applications of your competence and strengths for different class of users (e.g. organization, individuals, students, parents, old people, NGO's etc. Make a data base and classify possible user groups and find cost effective ways to interact with them (membership, telephones, email etc.)

3. Now prepare a list of key accelerators (resources which can be great facilitators for your GP).

Critical Decisions of the past

Have you ever noticed how sometimes we keep drifting from one idea to another unable to decide what we really want in life? However much of this happens because we do not have a general sense of direction of what we want to achieve in the long run and our specific desires keep on changing depending on what our neighbours or colleagues are doing. If our neighbour is searching for a house in the city, we start doing the same or if one of our colleagues has decided to enrol for a fellowship program we also start thinking of it. The result is constant confusion, rework and wastage of time and effort.

Since generic projects embodies the key aims of your life, you may like to test to find out the extent to which the specific decisions (that you have taken in the past) are in agreement with your GP.Think of the various critical decisions that you have taken in your life and now check whether they are in agreement with your GP (your Generic project as worked out in chapter III and then further refined in this chapter) using the format given below. You may think of really critical decisions such as taking a particular type of course/specialization, taking up a job, building your house, marriage etc and then see to what extent it is compatible with your GP.The idea of this exercise is to enable you to see whether the major decisions that you are taking in your life are in consonance with your GP and to examine the extent to which such decisions are supportive of generic projects.

Sl. No	*Decisions*	*+ / - (Impact to your GP)*	*Remarks*

- What can I do to mitigate the effect of certain Critical decisions that have a negative influence on my GP?
- What can I do to strengthen the effect of certain Critical decisions that have a positive influence on my GP?
- What future decisions may be taken for strengthening my GP?

Aligning your present to your GP

We often read success stories about successful people, who have thought big, taken bold decisions and made the most of their life and career. However for each of these successful people, there are many others who have ended up in failure and misery. Having big dreams is not bad but we must also ensure that we do not lose touch with our current reality. This is even more important in the present time of recession when people are losing jobs and there are fewer employment and growth opportunities. It is extremely important to pay attention to your current occupation and continue to grow strong in that. In some situations a prudent and cautious approach is very important just to survive these harsh times. However while managing this current reality let us also not lose sight of that which is of long term importance to our career. So, whatever be our situation we must still find time to nurture and strengthen our Generic Project, because that is what will provide us crucial advantage for long term growth and satisfaction in both career and life.

Just like a magnet is able to attract iron filing from its surroundings similarly a person of strong GP is able to attract the right kind of duties and responsibilities while being in a job or work situation. Sometimes it may involve the cooperation of the boss or superior but most importantly it requires clarity and initiative from you to it that more interesting work is assigned to you. The more you keep taking interesting work voluntarily, the more non interesting work (to you) starts getting assigned to someone else. However what is not interesting to you may be genuinely interesting to another to another whom it is assigned.

Task elements aligned to the direction of the generic project

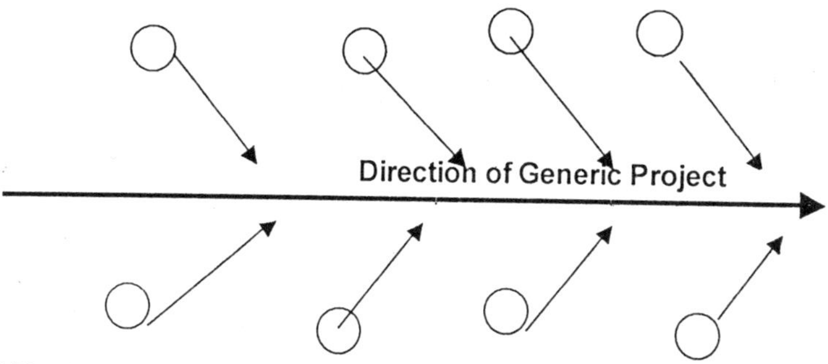

Aligning present work to your core strength-An illustration

A retired Principle once told me this real life story of a person who was a teacher in an elementary school and was declared as misfit for the teaching profession. This story goes something like this. As the news of Mr Kashyap's transfer to Govt. secondary school in Nainital spread, all sorts of gossip started flying. People discussed his habit of picking quarrels with other teachers, indiscipline in his class and numerous complaints from parents.

Even before his arrival there was so much adverse publicity about him that nobody wanted him to sit in their room. There were some senior teachers who even advised the principal to request the authorities to withhold his transfer to the school. So curious to know more the principal contacted his counterpart in Mr Kashyap's present place of posting.

He came to know more insinuating things about Kashyap-like he was all the time busy in running his shop and was not paying any attention to his school work. That he is good for being a petty shopkeeper and teaching can never be his cup of tea.

The CR and other service dossiers reflected the remarks of the superiors, which can be summed in a single sentence. He is complete misfit for a teacher.

However despite all this bad publicity about Mr Kashyap, the Principal decided to give him a chance, instead of losing all hope. According to him "I believe in the words of Shakespeare- Assume the virtues even if you can't find any. Since no one is prepared to sit along with him I decide to make his seating arrangement in my room". Finally Kashyap arrived and met the principal. He told him his side of the story. He had a very poor sense of self-esteem and blamed everyone else for his misfortunes.

In the words of the principal:

"I could see that he was not in the right frame of mind to do justice to his role as teacher at the moment. So I told him to forget what has happened and assured him that I would not go by what had happened in the past. So he can make a new beginning. I also told him to forget about his past CR and advised him to believe that he is going to do a wonderful job in his new job. Instead of giving him any regular teaching work, I asked him to tell me-what he was good at and his interest areas. And it came that he is very good at organizing functions etc. Since the annual function of the school was approaching, I asked him to take charge of all arrangements under my supervision. Here, he did a reasonable job. I was particularly impressed by his organizing skills, so I asked him whether he could help the school in construction of an approach road, which caused great inconvenience during the rainy seasons.

Here he showed his real talent, he could very easily organize the students for voluntary service and also get the required funds etc. After his grand success in this project, I assigned him teaching session and I was amazed to see 100 % attendance in his class and students taking keen interest. I personally sat through one of his classes and to tell you frankly found Mr kashyap to be above average, even better than some of the senior teachers who had advised me to stop his transfer to my school. So much about a man who was condemned to be misfit for the teaching profession Later Kashyap made a great career as a teacher."

Now look at this story from the Generic Project perspective. When the principal asked him to choose any particular activity he is good at. Kashyap opted for organizing cultural events which was his strength. This indicated his generic project to be in similar lines to a manager's work- which is organizing and coordinating the efforts of different individuals. Once he got hooked onto his generic project, he was able to rediscover his strength which had remained dormant in a set up where he was being given only teaching responsibilities. The respect of students and his colleagues, gave his self esteem a boost. Being resourceful he could quickly organize himself, go through the books which he had not referred to since ages and could do well as a teacher also.

Modifying Your Current Reality to Suit Your Generic Project

Your current reality i.e the type of work or occupation you are in, or your day-to-day activities for your survival and earning may or may not be in consonance with your generic project. It may also so happen that the daily routine may leave you very little time for your generic project. That is how; trapped in our daily existence, many of us learn to forget our dreams all together. Your generic project is an important device for you to modify your current reality to what is meaningful and important for you for your long term career growth. There is a prayer, which says – God give me the strength to change that which I can change in life and to bear with patience, that which I cannot change. The same principle applies here, even though you may not be able to change everything in life as described earlier to suit your GP, yet it may be possible to modify your current reality in a manner which suits your GP better.

Before we proceed further let us take a few minutes to review and reflect on your present work activities, with a view to aligning these to your Generic Project better. Make a brief note to yourself, while responding to each of the questions given below for your own reference and use later.

1. In what areas of my job do I excel? At what work in general do I excel?

2. What areas do I need to improve or develop? Do these areas hinder my ability to do a good job?

3. How do I manage "passing marks" in some areas which though not very important or long term are nevertheless important for my survival in present job/circumstances?

4. What kinds of assignments would I like to have this month/ quarter/ year including different or new work? What are my immediate or short term goals?

5. What work would I not like to be assigned to this month / quarter/ year, if possible?

6. What skills or knowledge is necessary to do the work I'd like to do? Is there someone I can ask?

7. Do I have these skills and knowledge presently? How strong am I or do I need to develop or strengthen this skills and knowledge?

8. What kinds of training or experience would I need to develop in these areas? How extensive would the training have to be?

9. Is it feasible for me to develop these skills? Revisit Q6. Look at your short-range goal. Are they realistic and attainable?

10. Keeping in mind my strengths (Q1), job opportunities in my field or organization, and the work I like, State what you think are your long term goals for (2-5 years).

11. What skills or knowledge are necessary to do the work defined in my long-range goal(s)?

12. Which of these skills and knowledge do I already have? What would I consider my level of competence to be?

13. What kinds of training/experience do I need to develop these skills? How much? How long will it take?

14. Is it feasible for me to develop these skills? Revisit Q11. Look at your long-range goal(s). Are they realistic? Plan a course of action.

Let us now see an illustration of how a person's ability to link his roles and responsibilities to his long term interest, facilitate better career growth and opportunities.

Illustration of a good fit between a person's roles/ responsibilities and his GP

Dipesh was a tall, physically strong and extrovert person who liked to travel and meet people. Apart from that he had keen interest in outdoor sports. Soccer was a favorite with him. During his college days he regularly participated in inter college tournaments, which also gave him an opportunity to travel to different parts of the country and meet different people.

After completing his graduation with great difficulty, he had to think in terms of a career. He knew very well that given his family circumstances he could not pursue his interest in football for too long. If we carry out an analysis using the Formats provided in this chapter, his generic project could be something like this-

> Gaining an edge thru interpersonal effectiveness and outdoor, adventurous activities etc.

After considering choices available to him, Deepesh decided to take up a one-year course on travel and tourism. His choice was partly governed by the fact that this was a short duration course and partly because this was readily available to him. After completing the diploma, Deepesh first took up a small job at a travel company specializing in adventure sports. Being a small company it gave Deepesh the opportunity to get an all round exposure in various gamuts of activities related to tourism and ticketing.

Though he was initially employed in the travel desk section, initiative to take additional responsibility during weekends got him the opportunity of working as guide to mostly foreign tourist. This helped him in developing good contacts with the prospective customer groups. His friendly nature came handy in developing relationships and in the long run he eventually started his own travel company which gave excellent results and was like a hobby to him.

Taking a cue from the above illustration, list all the activities, task, roles and responsibilities that are part of your current reality i.e your present job or work situation etc. Categorize them on the basis whether these are facilitating or hindering to your long term goals.

Activities /role / tasks etc.	*Whether Facilitating or Hindering to my GP*

Now work out an action plan to change your present activity profile so that it better supports your GP, by examining the following questions.

1. In what ways these activities provide learning opportunities and how can I further strengthen these to my specific requirements?

2. In what ways these roles and responsibilities provide networking opportunities with important people?

3. Which of these can be modified slightly so that they suit one or more of my GP perspective better? Which of these can be substituted by my favourite activity? What is the cost involved?

4. Is it possible to exchange responsibilities (with a colleague) to mutual satisfaction and advantage of both?

GP in an Era of Specialization

Many people say that this is an era of specialists and therefore we should be master of a particular skill or art. If you are a specialist in a particular field or wish to develop as one, your success in the long term will depend on the prospects of that particular specialization in future times to come. Being specialized in field is good but being highly specialized in a narrow field can be a liability for today of change. This is particularly true in present times, when the job situation is worsening due to economic down turn and recession. Look at what happened to some highly paying and specialized jobs such as merchant bankers, pilots etc in the past few months. Even in the best of time, when your particular field is growing you may be in great demand. However at other times there may not be many prospects for you. When a field of specialization looks promising every one gets into the bandwagon and soon the supply in the field is more than the demand. What therefore started as a promising career becomes hardly of any great potential for you in the long run? Your GP will help you in being flexible and willing to learn new things which provide you the strategic advantage for shaping your career to the best of your abilities and potential as well as the up coming new opportunities.

How GP will help you deal with Change

You might have observed many people go through transition in their career, which becomes painful and frustrating. They get into what can be termed as a neutral Zone-doing nothing worthwhile and waiting for the next wave of inspiration to come. Sometimes it is out of the formlessness of the neutral zone that new form emerges, just as out of the barrenness of the fallow time, new life forces take shape.

GP is important for our career, because genuine beginnings start with us, even when they are brought to our attention by external opportunities. Building a GP for your career growth is like having a constant purpose, a common thread in your work and professional life. It will make it possible for you to make the most of fallow time you get in your life, somewhat like a hobby akin to a professional interest which ensure that no matter what transitions you keep going through your life you are determined to make the most of it.

Hence, a flexible mind is needed to be able to rapidly refocus as you pass through transition times in life. In fact, a very good analogy to consider is how our eyes look at some particular new landscape. When we look at a new terrain, we typically let our eyes skip all around the field of view, focusing at each prominent landmark for a few seconds before moving on. At each landmark, the eye will focus at the correct distance for that landmark, even if it means letting other objects (at different focal distances) go out of focus for a little while. While our eyes are doing all of this, our brain automatically integrates all of the input so that we end up with a coherent mental model of what's out there. GP works in a similar way to help us develop the capacity to see the meaning and purpose of the whole by synthesizing a mental image through a collage of experiences, resources and abilities developed all through our development process.

Go ahead- Generate new choices and avenues of career Growth

Learning of this chapter is crucial for developing a wholesome perspective about work and career. Such a perspective will energize and nourish you for greater challenges. A well thought out GP will provide you with a clear focus, yet flexibility to adapt and prosper from the change in your work environment and situation. Most importantly it is going to the bridge between your career aspiration and "joy @work".

We talked about generating choices in the chapter on – mental models for higher latitudes. So here is a practical approach for generating the choices in these times of competition and change. As shown in the diagram below having a generic project means that you have a creative focus based on your core strengths and your specific circumstances.

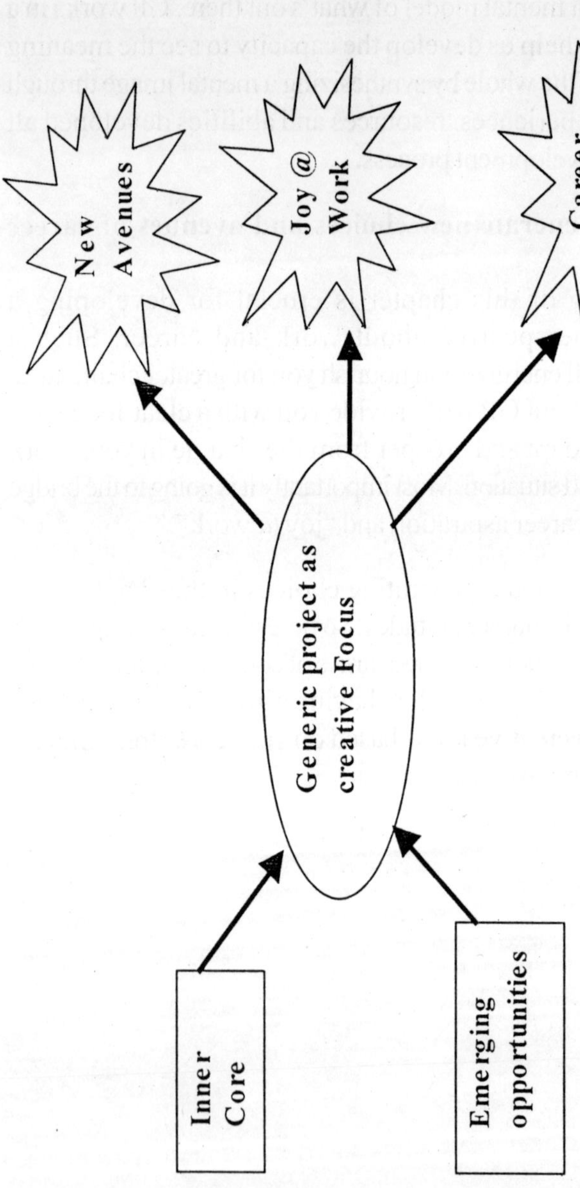

Fig. 4.2 Generic Project as Creative Focus.

5

Aligning Career Goals with Critical Roles

In the previous chapters we have discussed things, which mainly deal with our inner world. The concepts of mental models and generic projects help you in aligning your self with meaningful purpose of your life. However we have discussed very little about the external realities. The clarity and harmony of our inner world is often disturbed due to external factors and circumstances. Many spiritual gurus and their teachings help us in being in peace and harmony. There are also books that give us peace of mind and temporary relief.

Many people follow spiritual Gurus to get inspiration, harmony and peace in life, but unlike a sage or hermit, we can not live a life of recluse in the Himalayas. Believe me you need loads of money for that! Such ideas are of limited help when it comes to dealing with the external realities of our situation. We need to remember that all our achievements and results are mostly linked to our actions in dealing with the external reality. So we now need to talk about the skill of execution which is central to our ability to achieve our goals.

We are living in very interesting times. So much is happening around us – in the last 30 years or so there has been so much progress in science, technology that has not happened in the entire history of mankind. This quantum leap in complexity and pace of change can be experienced in every day life. We come to our work with some intentions, some ideas, ideals and role models of what we want to achieve but we are most of the times caught unaware, unprepared and unprotected in the face of too many happening around us at too fast a pace.

Excellence in the art of execution is nothing but mastering the art of harmonizing our inner world with the realities of external world and becoming increasingly confident in our abilities to generate the desired results in the present times of increasing competitive challenge. So what are the common responses? Faced with this complexity some of us simply withdraw. Some becomes workaholic-immersed in work all the time and some resorts to some form of addiction-watching TV, partying, socializing etc all the time. This takes it toll like a slow poison in our system-increasing monotony and progressively dimming our passions.

There are some-who start believing in the destiny and luck. All well till the time they run out of luck. Then there are those who sporadically plan their activities and goals, work out New Year resolutions once a while. Sometimes they do achieve what they had planned. However in the end it appears as though they had gone through a haze. There are times when they do achieve something and then wonder whether it is what they really wanted. Sometimes, by the time we reach our goal, the attractiveness of the goal itself diminishes so much, that it doesn't seem to matter much.

Finally there are those, I believe this number is not more than about 1% of our total human population, who believe in making systematic attempts. This involves systematically removing the haze or mystery from the process of achieving results- seeing the goals clearly all the time, evolving complementary and supporting goals and specific targets to reach there.

This 1 % of our human population does not comprise merely of celebrities or well-known public figure. But it comprises of many successful entrepreneurs-small or big, executives, professionals, specialists, artists, sports persons, students or housewives. There is an underlying similarity in their approach - there is a strong sense of reality, a sense of confidence that everyday they are becoming better at making sense of haze around them. This makes them confident of achieving results for themselves or for their near and dear ones. There is proper seriousness to take on the reality, a sense of humour and playfulness to enjoy the process while engaging in achieving results. You can now join this exclusive club and if you are already in, being still better at this art of execution. If you were a professional golfer, you wouldn't have liked to play in weather when there was lot of fog around in the golf course. Because then you wouldn't be able to know the difference between a good shot and a bad one and so, you wouldn't be able to gain the confidence in your abilities or wouldn't know as to how you may improve your handicap score.

That is the first thing about good execution. You can only learn the art of execution when you can see your goals clearly. Fortunately as a golfer you can always choose a place and time, when there is no fog and can enjoy and learn the art of golfing. But it is not so easy in real life, where there is lot of fog around us. Some of this fog is internal –i.e creation of our mind and some of this fog is external i.e. outside us and it also affects our thinking and decision-making and thus our ability to execute our goals.

The other day I met an HR professional in corporate set up of a large organization. While discussing his work with me, he said we are absolutely clear about our goals. Basically we make policies, implementation is not our role. It is up to the guys at the plant to ensure the implementation. Of course we can provide facilitation and support if required. Since he has disowned the implementation process, he will not be able to see the link between what he does and what results are derived by the organization. What ever he may say I am pretty sure that this HR professional, will loose his passion for learning and making a real contribution to the success of the organization.

The same way the entire aspect of life will become boring and academic without the adventure of execution. In fact execution is the only way in which you get into that state of flow, learning the implicit aspect, the finer aspects of the process of making it happen. Just like skill is knowledge in action, similarly execution is strategy and learning in action. You have to be deeply passionate about yourself and honest about your reality. It is the only way by which you develop your confidence and credibility in your career or profession or any other chosen field in which you wish to excel. Execution is much like driving or cycling, which you cannot do in a stationary position. You can only learn the art while moving. The guidance or mentoring has to be on-the job, during the process of execution.

Developing a Long Term Vision

Too many people assume that they know there long term goals with respect to their career etc. If some one asks you what would you be doing tomorrow or this week or next week, you would probably look into your dairy and say that. However if some one were to ask you what do you see yourself doing about a year later or so, then it would be difficult for you to answer that. Many people tend to just go by what others are doing or what seems to be the favourite bandwagon of their friends or colleagues. However if we do not evolve a long term vision for ourselves then there is every likelihood that we will get drifted in varied directions according to the exigency of the situation at the cost of long term satisfaction and growth.

All of us have dreams and aspiration about what we should achieve in our life and career. These dreams are often reflected in our vision, long term goals and plans that we have for future. When you look at your long term goals but do not feel fully committed, your vision is perhaps not in consonance with your values. Being aware about our own values is a key aspect of self awareness and is one of the most significant constituent for leading a stress free and happy life.

Values are deeply held views, of what we consider worthwhile. We receive these values from many sources: Early upbringing, parents, religious influence, schools, friends, teachers etc. Many are ingrained during childhood. We acquire others as adults. However, there's a distinction between "espoused" values, those which we presume that we believe in, and our "values in action", that is the value which actually influence our behavior. These latter values are embedded in our brains in such a way that we can't easily recognize them. We rarely examine or question them. That's why they create disharmony and conflict within us. Many spiritual gurus stress upon the importance of values and emphasize that we should beware of the temptation to let our values slip in difficult and testing times.

So here is an exercise that is designed to help you reach a better understanding of your most significant values, which will also help you to examine whether the decisions you have been making are in line with your espoused values.

Exercise: Aligning Vision with Cherished Values
Step 1: "What I value most"

One way to get in touch with our deepest feelings is by recalling any story or incident which you have found very inspiring and motivating. Take a few minutes to recall such stories or incidents and share these with a trusted friend or college. Discuss with your friend possible reasons as to why such a story is so inspiring to you. Ask your friend to identify aspects which could be the source of inspiration. Such aspects are likely to represent your values. Make a list of such Values and select three values that you hold most strongly, write the number 1 besides your pre-eminent value, 2 by the second most strongly held, and 3 by the third. Finally, in the same manner, rank orders the three that you reject most strongly. You may also refer to list provided in the excercise. My most significant values in Chapter 2, to help you identify values which you strongly hold as well those that you strogly reject.

Step 2

Take a look at the top three accepted values on your list.

(a) What do they mean, exactly? What are you expecting from yourself-even in bad times?

(b) How would your life be different if those values were prominent and practiced?

(c) What would an organization be like which encouraged employees to live up to those values?

(d) Does the personal vision, which you drew forth, reflect those values? If not, should your personal vision be expanded? Or are you prepared to reconsider your values?

(e) Are you willing to choose a life, and an organization, in which these values are paramount?

Now take a look at the top three rejected values on your list.

(a) What do they mean, exactly? What are you expecting from yourself-even in bad times?

(b) Have you faced any situation where there was a conflict of values –in the sense that the accepted values pointed to one direction, where as the rejected values pointed to the other direction?

(c) How did you resolve such dilemma?

(d) Are there any lessons which you would like to record and keep for future reference?

Step 3: Values and Career Decisions

Now that you have chosen your values think of the decisions that you have taken in the past and evaluate these decisions with respect to the extent to which these decisions have been aligned to your most important values. The diagram below shows the evaluation of a decision (enrolling for PhD) by a person with respect to his Values-both positive one's (i.e. those he cherishes) and negative one (i.e those he rejects)

The diagram in fig 5.1 illustrates a person for whom the 3 most important values are –Acquire knowledge, Intellectual status, and explore new ideas. Similarly the 3 rejected values for this person are –Money is more important than knowledge, Greater responsibility at work place, more time for family. Since both the sets of accepted values and the rejected values are in accordance to his decision of enrolling for PhD, this person will feel hardly any dissonance with respect to his decision. It will however be important for him to understand the implication of this decision on other aspects of career and life in general. Since his accepted Values are in accordance with the decision of enrolling for PhD, therefore these values will also facilitate a strong sense of motivation and commitment to his decision. Similarly the rejected values will act as enabler due to which he would be able to find the time for carrying out his research related studies etc.

Having gone through the above example examine 2-3 important decisions that you have taken in the last 5-10 years and examine to what extent these decisions were in accordance to your accepted and/or rejected values using a similar diagram that we have used above. In doing so first write out 2-3 Values which you strongly accept, then write out 2-3 values which you strongly reject and then use the diagram shown in above figure to see to what extent your decision is in accordance to your values and hence likely to be strong source of motivation for you.

Having completed the exercise, ask your self following question

1. Do I take decisions consciously and proactively or they just happen to me?

2. Are my key decisions (or lack of it) in accordance to my values?

3. Have I taken some decisions in the past that needs a thorough review?

4. How do I create strong motivation and commitment for my key decisions?

The art of seeing your goals clearly

There is an instance in the great Indian epic Mahabharata, which illustrates the importance of seeing your goals clearly. During

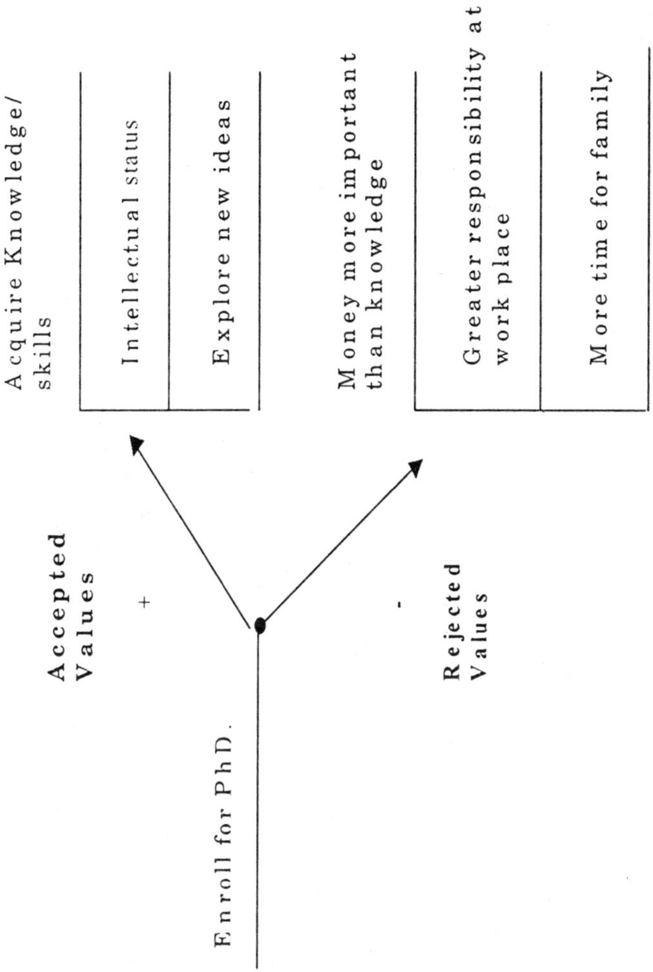

Fig 5.1. Values and Career Decisions

the training period of the heirs of the royal family, their mentor cum trainer dronacharya takes them for the archery lessons. He asks each of the prince to aim for the eye of the bird perched on a treetop. While they aim at the targets, he asks them-what are you seeing? So each one replies as per his perception. Yudhister says he can see the sky, the tree and the bird sitting on the branch. Similarly Duryodhan says he can see a bird sitting slightly hidden beneath the branches etc. However when it comes to Arjuna, the great archer and disciple of dronachraya, Arjun says – "I see only the eye of bird ". No wonder Arjuna went in to become the greatest archer playing a decisive role in the battle of Mahabharata.

This small story from Mahabharata shows the importance of seeing your goals clearly. It is one of the most important and fundamental things for the purpose of execution. However, unlike a structured training setting, seeing your goals clearly in real life is much more demanding and skilful job. In this constant endeavour to lead a meaningful and purpose driven life, we are constantly engaged in setting and achieving goals or targets.

Out of these goals or targets some are of our own choosing and are very close to us, some are given to us by others, some arise out of a situation and like the evening tide vanish by the first ray of the sunshine. Some seem far away and distant for too long, appears hazy for long and then suddenly appear in the horizon, tantalizing and challenging us with compelling possibilities for future. So how do we deal with these myriad possibilities of our life? Setting specific goals and objective is therefore the first and foremost challenge in developing the skill of execution.

Significance of Roles

The significance of role in a situation is very well illustrated in an anecdote from Mahabharata. At the successful completion of the training of royal heirs, a function was organized for the display of their warfare skills. The king and other members of Royal were present in this function. Each prince was asked to display their skills after introducing them to the noble gathering. Each prince came to the arena and described their identity, giving all details about their title, their royal lineage and so forth.

However when the turn of Arjuna came, he described himself only as Drona Shishya (Disciple of Guru Drona). So, the prime minister asked him - is this your only identity? and Arjuna replies emphatically – Yes this is my only identity. He clarifies that there can be confusion because of multiple identity, therefore I wish to retain only this identity-that of a true disciple of my Guru Drona (from whom he had learnt the art of archery). This incident shows his dedication to his role as a learner of the art of archery, a true disciple of Drona. No wonder he went on to become the greatest archer in the world. Though in today's time it may be difficult even for a student to excel only in one particular role, in complete disregard to other roles; yet this story illustrates the importance of critical roles in various point of time of our career.

Your generic Project and meaningful goals

The generic project that you have worked out, gives you a broad direction for deciding on various aspects of your career

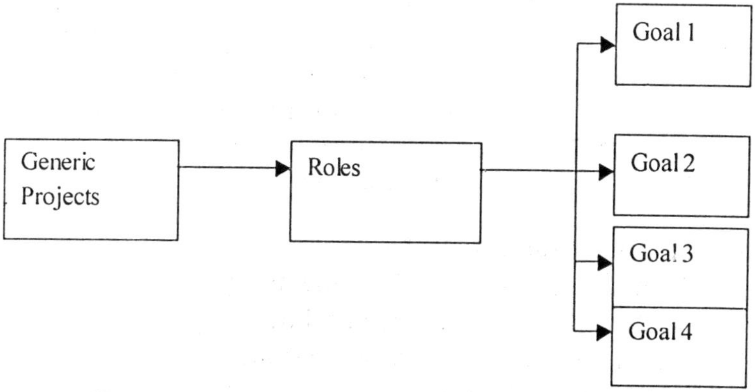

Fig 5.2.: Generic Projects, Roles and Goals

and professional issue. But that in itself cannot guide you in working specific goals and objective in your daily life. Setting specifies goals require understanding of your current reality or situation. It is not always possible to dream for an ideal, when your first priority needs to be to avoid the worst. Your response has to take into account of the situation in which you find your self. We will now apply the concept of strategic thinking to develop a process for setting specific and meaning full goals.

Examining Critical Roles for deciphering meaningful goals

Our Goals are not stand alone entity, which appear only as a result of our wishful thinking. They are interwoven around our own expectations and the expectations of significant others around us. Have you observed this irony, that it becomes increasingly difficult for us to achieve our own objectives, when we become too narrowly focused on them, without being sensitive to the expectations of others?

In our day-to-day life we are required to take on different roles. These roles are broad generalization of what is expected of us – as say head of family, parent, a professional, supplier, superior, subordinate etc. These roles are important for us, because we need to take into account expectations (our own / and significant others) while formulating our goals. We need to do this so that we can we can negotiate win-win strategies, get cooperation, time, resource and other support for our own strategic goals.

Exercise: Seeing Goals through the prism of Roles

In this exercise, we shall learn a process of evolving specific goals by examining our critical roles through a series of steps.

Step 1: Understanding Roles

In the first step list out all the roles that you need to take on periodically to be effective person, while doing and include all kinds of roles such as Work & professional roles, Family and social roles, personal roles etc.

Sl. No.	*Roles*	*How they are important to you in dealing effectively with your current reality*

Step 2: Identifying Critical Roles

Using the matrix given in the next page, rate the extent to which each of your role influences other roles and your Generic project, using the scale 1-neglible influence to 4-utmost influence. The matrix is just a hypothetical example for a person who has recently left a public sector organization to join a large private sector company.

Now select 3- 5 critical roles, which have an overbearing influence upon all other roles as well as your generic project also. The above is an example for a working professional, you may create a similar matrix for yourself as a student or business person etc.

Understand clearly your own expectations and expectation of significant other in these critical roles

Step 3

The role of an individual at any level in any organization is driven by the expectations of other significant related roles for that particular position, e.g. the role of a student is to a very large extent determined by the expectations of his teachers, parents and professionals in his chosen field. Similarly the student may in turn also have expectations from these various roles as well as his own role. Therefore harmonizing these expectations from each other becomes important for meeting your goals through the co-ordinated effort and cooperation of all.

Identifying Critical Roles

Roles	*Extent to which the role influences other Roles and is critical for Success of your GP (Give Rating 1 to 4)*						
	A	*B*	*C*	*D*	*E*	*GP*	*Total Points*
A. Head of family							
B. General manager							
C. A new joinne in a large company Subordinate							
D. Father							
E. Investor							

As a student or professional the different roles with which you need to interface in that position determine the roles of an individual. For any person to understand his / her role, it is important to:

- Identity the various interfacing roles w.r.t your role and categories into various groups.
- Understand the expectations of each interfacing role.
- Understand and identify conflicting expectations of different roles.
- Understand the importance of each group for organizational effectiveness and negotiate those needs to arrive at a balance.
- Execute and implement to meet the needs.
- Constantly assess and rebalance the emerging and conflicting needs.

An Example of My Partners at Work: for a student preparing for a competitive examination

Please remember that this is just an example, you can create your work sheet as per your specific requirements. Pl. mention in

My parents or guardians	*My class mates or friends*

ME

Teachers/mentors	*Librarian/ Sr. students etc*

the format below type of support each of the group need from you and Type of Support you need from them

1. What are the conflicting expectations of other groups and how I can resolve these by negotiating with each of these groups to strike a balance between different priorities?

Group 1 (Parents/ Guardians)

___

___

___

Group 2 (Teachers/Mentors)

___

___

___

Group 3 (friends / Colleagues)

___

___

___

Group 4 (Librarian / Tutors / Sr.students etc)

___

___

___

2. What steps I need to take to develop a work group for joint study, exchange of books/notes/ resources etc who share the passion for excellence in my chosen field.

3. What steps I need to take to develop my support group for giving me feedback on my progress, clarifying doubts, providing resources etc.

Step 4

Now, against each of the critical role examined by you above, write specific goals for effective performance on that Role.

Sl.No	*Critical Roles*	*Specific Goals*

Step 5: Creative Visualization

Redefine your goals using a creative process describe below. Now ask yourself

- Are there goals, which I have just taken upon me at the instance of others or a matter of habit but they do not contribute, to effectiveness in any of my critical roles?
- Are there goals, which are significant to more than one Role?
- Are the learning's and experience of achieving one particular goal is likely to have bearing on my effectiveness in other roles in future?
- To what extent this goal will be helpful in dealing with my current reality?
- To what extent this goal is useful for my Generic project?
- Do others rigidly define the Goals for me or can I modify or substitute it so as to achieve the desired results?
- Are there goals which compete with each other or they are complementary to each other?
- Is it possible to modify the goals to make them more complementary or supplementary to each other?

- Is it possible to merge two goals into one?

Step 6: Redefined Goals with Relative Priorities

After analyzing the above questions, redefine your goals and assign them specific priorities, by taking into account the timing aspects also that is specifying the most suitable time period for executing those. In the timing consideration, you may also identify such triggering events, which can make your goals more urgent, compelling or worthwhile.

Sl.No	*Specific Goals*	*Relative Priority*	*Timing Considerations*	*Remarks*

Some More Aspects to Make Your Goals Compelling

Only the goals that are well formed and specific are compelling. Such goals have a great motivational influence in you. So let us see how we can make our goals compelling.

Getting the evidence for Your Goal Fulfillment

How would you know whether you have achieved your goal? Some people are never sure whether they have achieved their goal or not. That is because they do not have a way of measuring their progress, so they cannot say whether their day-to-day behavior is taking them closer or farther to their cherished goals. Sometimes, it is possible that though they are achieving their goals, yet they may never get the feeling of satisfaction of achieving something.

For example if you have joined a new company, one of your goals may be to be successful in the new job. However if you don't have any sensory specific evidence i.e. - what you will see, hear or feel, so that you know you are successful. You may work a lot and put in great effort but you would never know whether you are truly succeeding in your job or not. Make sure that the goals you have listed in above step are specific manner that is possible to get realistic feedback on the evidence regarding whether you are achieving the goal or not. State the goal with specific such as –

- What will I see, hear or feel on achieving the goal?
- What is the intermediate feedback I could be receiving?
- What are some low hanging fruits or positive reinforcement that I am likely to get within short term if I am progressing in the desired manner?
- What are some intermediate goals or steps, which give me feedback on my progress?
- Define your present state as specifically possible and then see what difference will come to you as you march forward in your journey

Sharing Your Goals with Significant Others

The path to achieving your goal does not necessarily have to be a lonely or solitary one. You can enlist the support of your near and dear ones or those with who you are not in an adversarial or competitive situation. It is also possible that you may not consider involving some people in your goals. It always becomes easier when you know. It is so much easier to achieve your goal when you are careful about where, when and whom that goal is important. If you want a goal to spread over to the entire fabric of your life, consider where in your life it will make the most difference and begin there.

Checking the Ecology of Your Goals

Some time we get so obsessed with our goals that we may loose track of the rest of our lives. It is something like the story of Midas, Who after getting the boon of Midas touch turns everything into gold and then finds his life devoid of any joy of relationship, feelings etc. It is important to see in what manner the changes will affect your life and relationships. A job at a Higher Salary or responsibility may look very attractive but you also need to consider things such as- Will it change my relations with colleagues, friends, or family. Will I be able to give the same attention to my child etc? Discover the difficulties that are produced as a result of fulfillment of your dream, not to dissuade you from them but to allow you in advance to prepare for them. How can I adjust, refine or adjust my goals further so that what might have been a negative consequence becomes a positive opportunity.

Exercise: Visualizing a Compelling Future

1. Imagine watching a movie of your own success
2. See your self in the future performing the role of your choice
3. Make sure that your goals are clear and compelling to you
4. Make your images compelling with special effects
5. Notice the pathway from present to that compelling future

Examining Alternate Goals and Pathways for Realizing the Vision

When you wish to develop a long term vision for your career, think about it in detail. Try to look at some of your dreams and aspirations. What sort of career you aspire for? Look at this from all the 3 perspectives of What? Why ? And How? It is not only important to just say what do you want but you must also try to

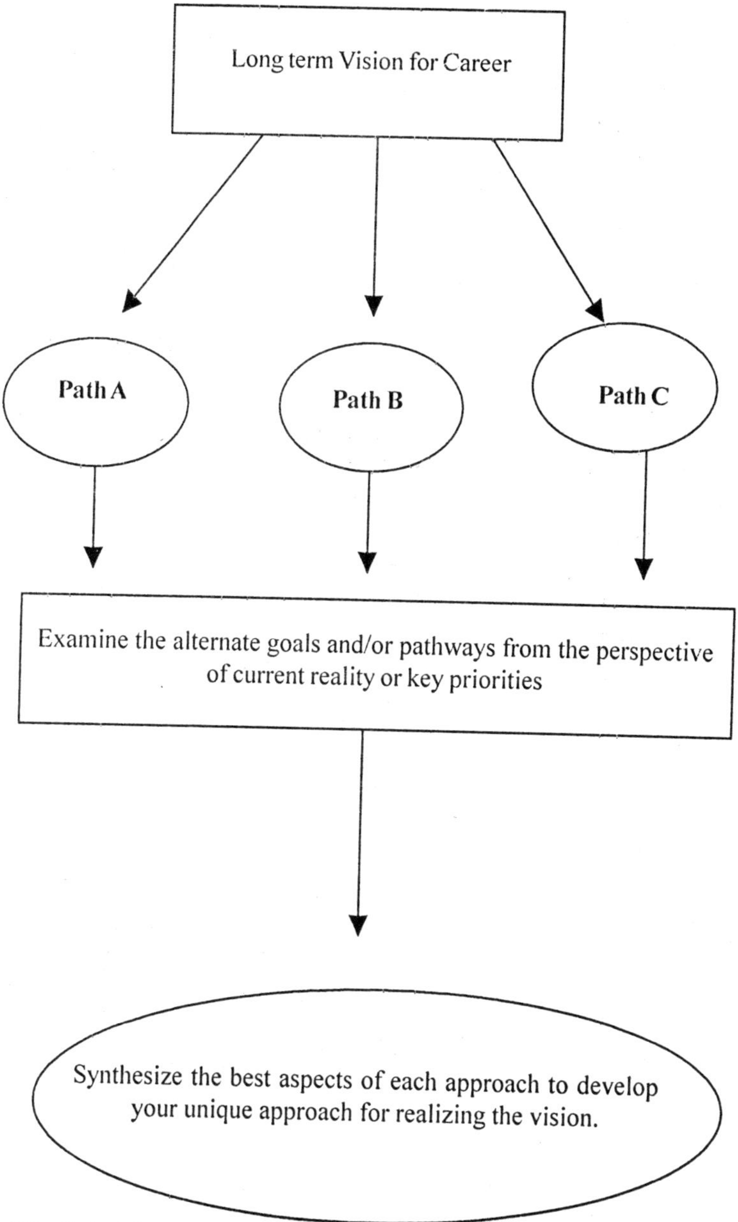

Fig 5.3. Alternate Goals or pathways for achieving the career vision

answer the question of why? Why is such a vision important for me? Is this vision in line with my cherished values or Is it connected to my generic project and will help me achieve long term satisfaction or is this just something which I have to do to make good money for the time being? Once you have made up your mind about this broad long term vision about your career, think about alternative approaches to realize this vision. This is illustrated in the diagram in the next page.

Once the long term vision is understood, one can think of possible pathways to achieve those. There may not be a single pathway but many an alternative ones which could lead to the same broad types of results that you are looking for. Suppose you wish to make a career out of your passion for flying. Then there can be various alternative paths to achieve this. Say by joining Air force or by getting a license as commercial pilot or being a navy pilot etc. How to conceive a pathway that is suitable to our temperament, resources and situations is often crucial for achieving success.

Disney Creative Process

You will be surprised to know that Walt Disney Company - now a mega-empire with profits of the order of $1.3 billion was the creation of a high school drop out who suffered bankruptcy and repeated financial and business disasters. Would you not like to know, how one man could overcome all the obstacles to become a legend?

Walt Disney's creative abilities and success can be summarized in one word: Imagineering. The term, coined by Disney in 1967, combines the words "imagination" and "engineering." Walt Disney used to follow a conscious strategy to draw out creative ideas and then convert these ideas into workable projects. It is said that Walt Disney used to consciously play three roles while working on a project. These roles are: the Dreamer, the Realist, and the Spoiler (the Critic).

The Dreamer: (WHAT)

As the term indicates the Dreamer looks at the big picture with an open mind that anything is possible. It largely involves visual imagination and experiencing a future desired state through all of your senses, as if you are seeing a movie of your own success in the future.

The Realist: (HOW)

The fantasies about the future are then made real by associating the feelings of imaginary characters and acting them out (as in rehearsal) to give them life just like in a drama. The process of 'realizing' the dream may also include creating several short stories which leads to dream through a series of steps. This also involves trying out the "imaginary steps" in different sequences and combinations. The realist work with a strong belief that the dream is possible and focuses on building a series of successive approximations of actions that are required to actually fullfill the dream.

The Critic: (WHAT IF, with Focus on Chance to Improve)

Disney's process of critical evaluation involved disassociating himself from the project and examining it from the other's point of view. The Critic takes a dispassionate 'second look' from the point of view of a third person. The Critic arises as a result of taking a second look at one's creations from the position of a critical audience. The critic main role is to help in removing the hurdles and bottlenecks by logically applying different levels and types of criteria. Through internal dialogue the Critic examines, how the idea or plan holds up under various possible future scenarios.

The **Dreamer** is necessary for generating innovative ideas and goals with an attitude that anything is possible.

The **Realist** is necessary for generating options as a means to transform ideas into concrete and practical steps.

The **Critic** is necessary for taking a more dispassionate look, not to stifle the creativity but to find ways to improve the action plan, so as to avoid problems and ensure quality.

An idea may go through several iterations between the 3 phases i.e. Dreamer phases to Realist to the Critic phase, so as to improve the action plan An idea is finally taken up for implementation only when the Critic can not find any more loopholes.

Exercise: Applying Disney creative Strategy to examine alternative pathways to the same goal

Disney creative strategy can be applied to examine the suitability of various pathways to achieving the same goal. In the dream phase look at the possible scenarios for achieving your long term goal or a cherished dream. Then in the realist phase look at alternate pathways for achieving this goal and try to visualize the approximate steps or actions that would be required if you follow that particular path to your goal.

In the critic phase look at the entire approach from a critic point of view, including various contingency situations that can lead to problems, with the basic idea of using a modified approach so as to make your plan more robust and less susceptible to any contingencies that may arise.

When you follow this approach to alternate pathways it is always possible to synthesize a new pathway that embody the best of every other pathway in a manner to ensure better results for you. So here is yet another exercise to enable you to practice this approach for realizing your long term goals.

This exercise is aimed at providing an actual experience of the Disney creative process applied to a real life situation. This could be achieving a goal or solving a problem.

1. Close your eyes and think of an important goal that you would like to achieve in about 2 to 3 years time frame. This goal could be professional or personal or family related etc as per your priorities.

2. Begin with end in mind. Try to "see" the final images or scenarios (i.e. pictures) as you see in a movie, clearly showing the state of affair after you have already achieved the desired outcome in relation to this goal.

3. Now give a "title" to this final scenario (as described in the above para). Write this title in a blank sheet of paper and find out who else are interested or knowledgeable about your area of interest.

4. Think of 3- 4 alternate scenarios or pathways by which you could achieve your long term goal. Describe each of these pathways in your own word in separate paragraph and give a subtitle to each of these. For e.g if promotion to a higher level position is your preferred long term goal, you may consider pathways such as promotion in present organization or getting a higher level job outside present organization or even a prestigious offshore assignment (which may have long term significance for your career.)

5. Look for who all are passing by that pathway and what are their experiences. What are hurdles in each pathway and what are the opportunities. Preferably form a reference group who have past experience of traversing similar pathways and learn from their experience.

6. Select a pathway which suits your requirement, temperament, resources and above all which is in accordance to your generic project and then work out a detailed plan as to how to achieve the specific outcomes. You may also synthesize a new pathway by combining elements of known pathways. Play the dreamer, realist, critic role intensely as in Disney creative process one by one.

- **Dreamer- Imagining what is possible.**
- **Realist- Planning how to reach.**
- **Critique- Evaluating the plan according to key Values and looking for problems and missing links**

7. While playing the role of critique, dissociate yourself from the goal and instead consider that this goal is that of somebody else, someone who is similar to you in resources, temperament etc (let us say Mr X) and then look at all the hurdles that can come in your pathway to modify or improve your plan so that your plan is realistic and achievable.

Mapping Your Progress for Excellence

Once you have set about some goals you must have a map regarding the type of competencies and behavior that you will need to pursue these goals in a sustained manner for achieving the results. The exercise given below will help you asses your progress with respect to the progress in terms of competencies and the resources you need for achieving the goals.

Planning and Organizing, Well-being and Hassle free ness, Role efficacy, Networking and support Index

Listed below are a list Core Competencies and typical work behaviors that are helpful in mastering desired execution skills. Pick out 2 behaviors from each competency that you feel are of the highest importance to your job. Using a Rating of 1-4 rate the amount of training you need to improve in that behavior.

[1---------------2------------------3------------------4]
Little more still more large

See the example below:

Creative Thinking

Rating

4____ Solving problems creatively

_____ Creating new ways to improve quality, efficiency or other gains

_____ Creating different ways of doing a task

2____ Thinking in terms of what is possible

_____ Being able to apply creative-thinking to your job

Your turn...

Creative Thinking

Rating

_____ Solving problems creatively

_____ Creating new ways to improve quality, efficiency or other gains

_____ Creating different ways of doing a task

_____ Thinking in terms of what is possible

_____ Being able to apply creative-thinking to your job

Flexibility/Adaptability

Rating

_____ Looking for better ways to "the way we've always done it"

_____ Remaining calm in high-pressure situations (i.e. disappointments)

_____ Adapting your style to the needs of employees and co-workers

_____ Setting priorities for handling key areas and responsibilities as needed

_____ Dealing effectively with fears of change

Networking Effectiveness

Rating

_____ Empathizing and listening to others

_____ Able to network with concerned people on areas of mutual interest

_____ Sharing information and being upto date on important developments

_____ Managing disagreements effectively,

_____ Keeping commitments and helping others

_____ Consulted by others on important issues or problems

Planning and Organizing

Rating

_____ Understanding your key strengths, vision and generic project

_____ Being able to speak in a positive way about your values and strengths

_____ Planning and organizing for resources

_____ Understanding critical roles for your success

_____ Generate and share resources to obtain the best value

Well being and hassle freeness

Rating

_____ Planning each day's work with enthusiasm

_____ Managing health (physical/emotional) effectively and maintaining high energy level.

_____ Self driven and participating in self-development activities

_____ Free from excessive burden of loan or unrealistic expectations of others

_____ Learning from feedback of significant others and constantly improving.

_____ Practice hobbies/activities which rejuvenate self regularly

Systems Thinking

Rating

_____ Understanding systems and practices in my work environment and how it can be helpful for my career.

_____ Understanding relevant systems and procedures in your work environment

_____ Being able to explain how one's work contributes to the my family/work group

_____ Understanding the roles and responsibilities of others in one's work group

_____ Knowing how your role relates to others in the family/ organization/work group etc

Technical Skills

Rating

_____ Demonstrating operational and technical skills related to your career field

_____ Maintaining high standard of knowledge and skills in your chosen field of interest

_____ Using available technology effectively (e.g. computer softwares, email, mobile etc.)

_____ Assuring a high level of safety and quality in the workplace

_____ Participating in measuring outcomes of work

Please use the space provided below to mention specific areas where you may needs further support through training / coaching /mentoring/networking etc.:

____

____

____

Work out an action plan to acquire the competencies in areas which are most important to your GP.

6

Identifying Latent Patterns Inhibiting Growth

Whenever we embark on the journey of achieving our career goals, we also set in a growth process for our own development. But many a times you will observe that as you set in the growth process, a limiting process also seem to materialize in a manner quite similar to Newton's third law of motion, which says "Every action has an equal and opposite reaction". So while you turn on the growth process for your career growth and development, there also sets in a limiting process which tends to limit or oppose your growth.

Let us understand this limiting process through an illustration. When you sow a vegetable seed in your kitchen garden, the process of plant growth starts as you put in effort in terms of watering the plant, putting manure etc. As the plant grows a little and starts sprouting, the limiting process also starts. This is often in the form of insects, which starts feeding on the leaves, thereby harming the plant growth. If you now wish to ensure the growth, you will need to spray insecticide. The insecticide will kill the insect but it may leave some harmful effects on the plant or vegetable. Now just imagine that if you could have foreseen this limiting process and taken expert advice before sowing the seed, you could have selected insect resistant seeds so that the negative effects of limiting process would have been minimized or eliminated.

Your career or professional growth is also affected by a similar limiting process, which is often latent or invisible. It is a paradox that when we are putting all efforts in our career, we tend to lose out on health or relationships etc. When we are busy earning a lot, we have hardly any time to care for our family or enjoy the wealth; but when we do have lot of money it doesn't seem to matter much.

If at all we could anticipate the possible down trends elsewhere, when we were still going strong, then it would be possible for us to avoid the trap of limiting process that is waiting for us. It is utmost important for us to identifying such pattern which may be silently operating in our life and affecting our growth. When you become aware of these limiting processes, you can work out appropriate approaches and strategies to break the negative spiral of the limiting process, while also reinforcing the positive spiral of growth. We will now see some of such latent processes which tend to limit our growth or create hindrances in our progress. Some typical limiting processes that are applicable in case of career growth are given below.

Nothing Grows for Ever

As a student you would have observed that by putting in more efforts you can improve your marks. But the amount of effort that you had to put to improve your scores from 70 to 80 % is much higher than that when you tried to improve it from 60 to 70%. When you reach 90%, you need to put extremely high effort to even gain 1 more extra percentage. A point then comes where you seem to have hit the limit for whatever effort you put in, you

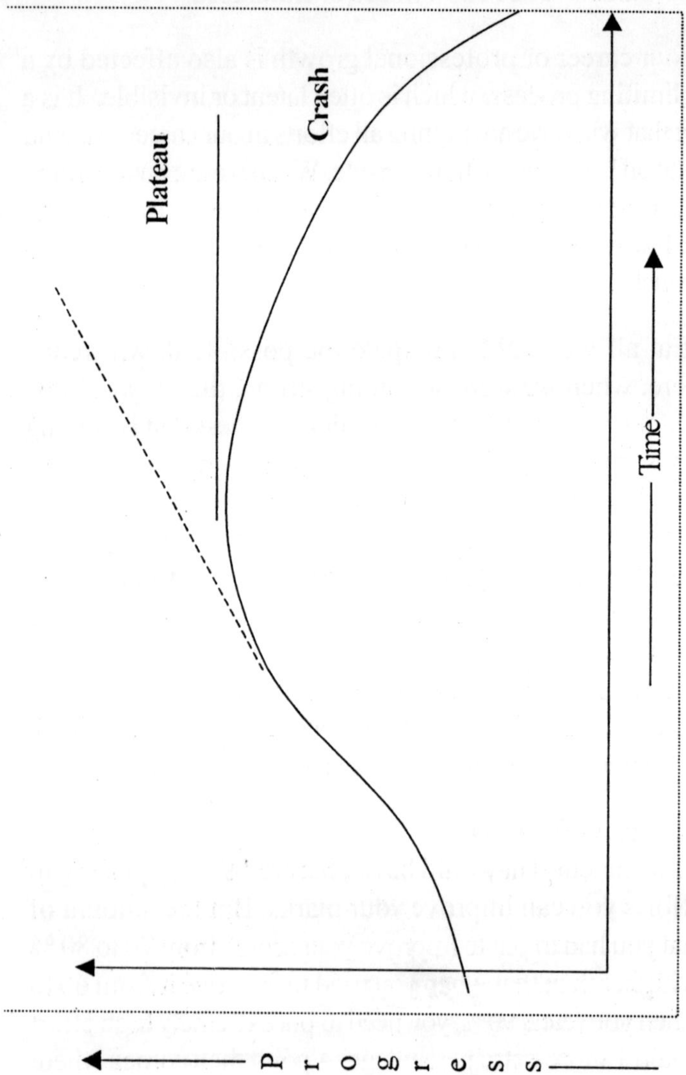

Fig. 6.1. The Plateau Effect.

do not seem to cross that level. Same is true for any career situation. The initial progress is quite rapid but then you seem to hit a plateau. If you feel that you have suddenly hit a wall or a ceiling then the plateau effect may be playing a part in your life. When you start on a new endeavor, the initial progress is fast but then the growth rate depreciates. This is shown in the Fig 6.1 in the previous page.

Your obvious response is to increase the effort, put more resources and so on but now the harder you push, the situation seem to conspire against you and push you back with more and more vigour. You may find one of the two things happening – either you hit the plateau, where your growth levels off or there is a rapid decline leading to an eventual crash. Hitting the plateau is a clear sign that more of what you are doing will not improve the situation. Simply putting in more effort only increases the sense of frustration and leads to demotivation and loss of creativity. It is better to learn to relax and reflect rather than to spend all your energies with more and more effort.

The plateau effect is very important for parents of young children, who wish to guide their children in their career. A common scenario for highly progressive parents is this- parents start emphasizing discipline and long hours of study, even when the child is in lower classes say below class IX. The child gets higher grades in lower classes because the syllabus ie easy, however as he goes to higher classes the grades level off or start declining. The child is pushed to extremes with tuitions/coaching classes etc to score high marks. They continue to do well say upto class IX or X, but when the time comes for real push in class XII, the child is so bored and frustrated that the plateau effect comes into the play and may even lead to a rapid decline.

A better strategy for the parents is to let the child enjoy the studies, as well as continue to do regular work. Emphasis should be in developing interest and self discipline and not only in getting high grades and then when the child is in higher classes like XI and XII, more support in terms of resources/ coaching etc should be given so that the child is able to take up the challenge. A similar pattern is also identifiable in parents who make their child dependent on them all the time. This may be termed as boomerang effect.

Boomerang Effect

In many schools children are given some projects to help them develop interest and concepts in various subjects. These projects are also graded and contribute to the final grade of the student. Many parents do the project on their own instead of letting the child take his own initiative, so that the child gets a high rating. The learning is therefore to the parent and the child loses the opportunity to learn and discover things by his own initiative.

Though the child continue to get good grades as a result of the parents doing the project, he/she does not absorb the learning and learn the art of problem solving through his own initiative and this affects the child's sense of self confidence in the long run. In fact the student projects are an excellent vehicle for helping the child discovers his potential and abilities. It is helpful in strengthening his generic project because in this process the child learns to marshal resources, cooperate with other students and solve the problem on his own initiative. However in the pursuit of short term goal of getting good marks for the project, the parents often compromise on the long term gain for the child's development. This is shown in Fig 6.2.

Crowd Spoils the Party

A person interested in setting up his shop in his neighbourhood observes that there is great need for a tailoring shop. So he sets up a tailoring shop as a business proposition. Initially he does good business because there is no competition in

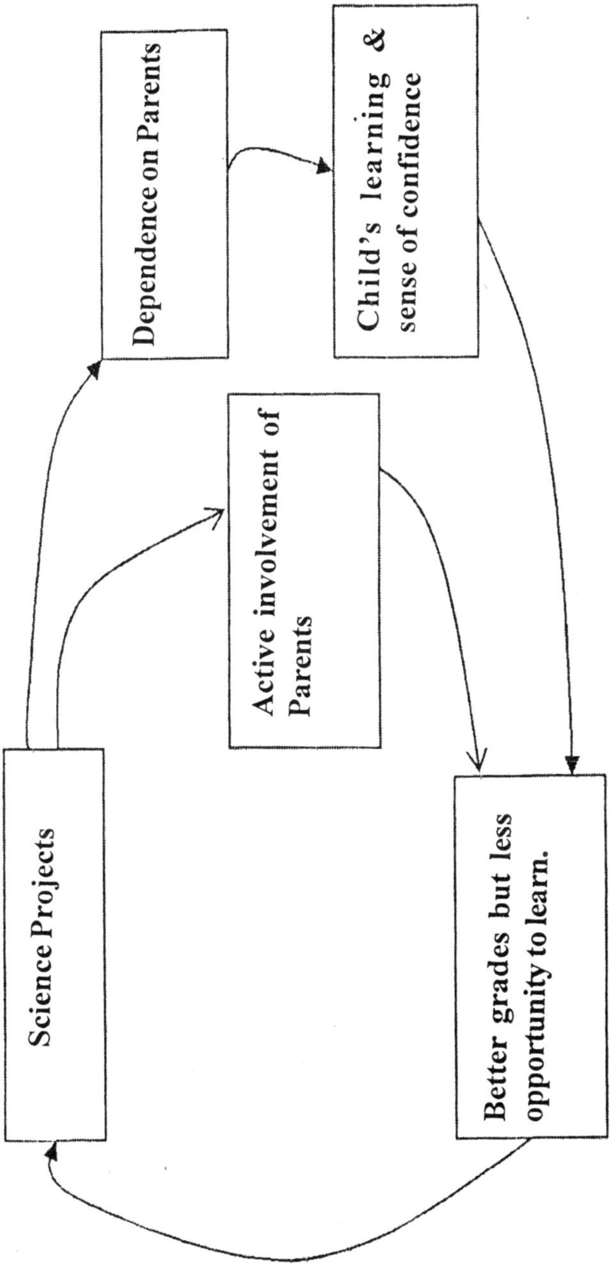

Fig. 6.2. Short term gains jeopardizing the long term benefits

that segment. Soon many other shop owners realize that this is a good business opportunity and they also set up tailoring shops. They start undercutting each other and finally the business is no longer attractive.

A similar thing happens in the field of career. A new branch of engineering is offered. It has good potential, so every body starts opting for it. Now there are so many qualified professional in that field that the supply exceeds the demand. This is shown in Fig 6.3.

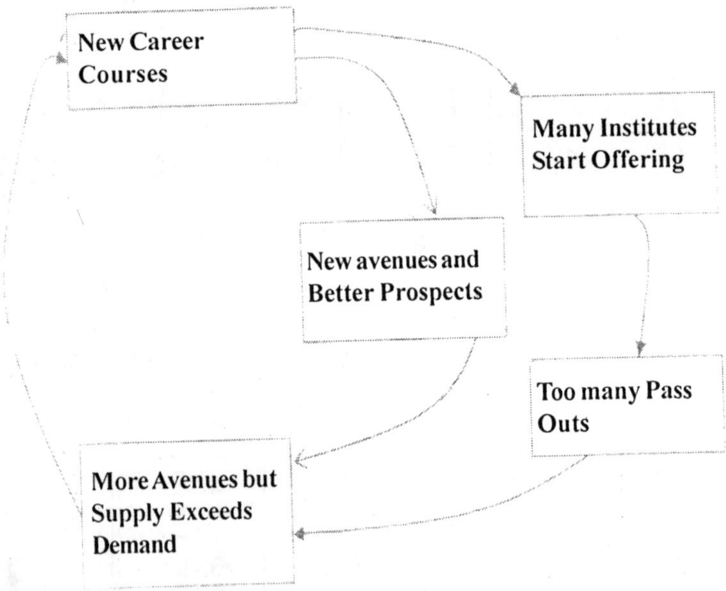

Fig 6.3. Crowd Spoils the Party

My Rise Seem to Trigger Your Down Fall

There was an interesting TV serial – "kamzoor kadi kaun". Its English equivalent could be titled as – "who is the weakest link". This TV show demonstrate the human tendency in group situation. The participants in this game show always conspire to remove the best candidates - who in reality are the strongest resources of the group. Something similar happens in real life too-when ever we work in teams we tend to discount the poor performer as well as the best performer in the group. This is because the group tends to like the people who are average. Another psychological reason for this is that the members of the group feel inadequate in the presence of extremely strong person amongst them and it evokes the feeling- "your rise seems to trigger our downfall". This leads to a silent understanding among others that you are the source of their misery and so they start conspiring (sometime in not a very overt or evident manner) for your downfall.

The lesson in this latent pattern is that whenever you are in a such a situation in your work place or college etc., always down play your achievements or success so that you do not trigger in the feelings of inadequacy in others. A somewhat similar pattern which may block our growth is in situation where the –solutions to your problems are nightmare for others. This often leads to a win-lose pattern eventually leading to lose-lose.

Partnership that goes sour

Some times it is useful to form partnership for mutual gain in career growth or problem solving. There are many problems or situations in real life including that of career that can be better handled through forming partnerships. Though partnership and strategic alliances are of great value but it is also true that there are also times when we feel betrayed by it. One of the reasons for this is that, we rush in to trust others and form a partnership without understanding the motives of the other person. It is said that the Japanese firms place a lot of importance on partnership. But this partnership is build gradually over a period of time, with small joint ventures first to test the strength of the partnership. When they get convinced about each other utility they form lasting relationships. The same is true with building real value long term partnerships- go slow in the begining and then gradually discover the combined strength of your partnership.

Critical Constraints

The effect of critical constraint is evident in situations where you tend to increase your work load to maximize your gain. The gain may be anything from earning more money to getting more appreciation etc. As you keep expanding your workload, the work pressure increases and may increase the chance of careless mistakes or over commitment or say not being able to deliver the quality in a timely manner. This may increase the output but decreases quality in and satisfaction of those who matter- customer, boss or colleague's etc.This in turn reduces your credibility and lead to reluctance in assigning you important work. I am not suggesting that one should not try to expand work to gain more results for self but it is also very important to be aware of the limiting process so that you may learn to think of creating ways to optimizing your overall gain and satisfaction rather than reacting with more and more effort which does not necessarily give you more results.

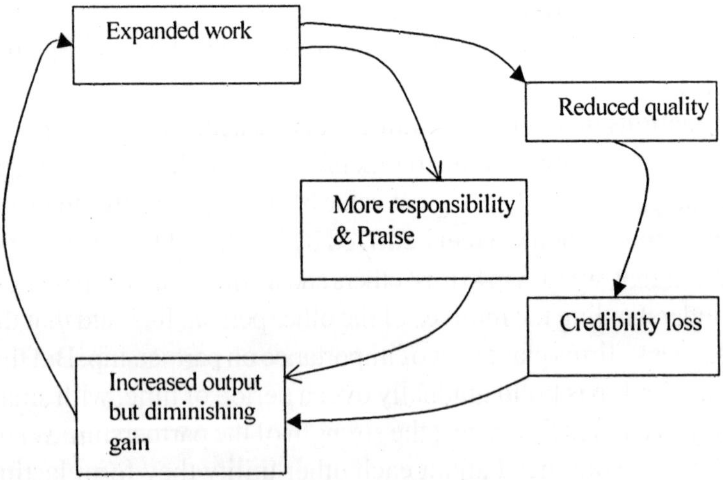

Fig. 6.4. Critical Constraints

Normally if you are not careful the impact of deteriorating quality or errors will not be evident to you for sometime. This is the invisible loop which you come to know after a long time. This is illustrated in Fig 6.4.

Another very common example of constraints to growth is when an excellent teacher is promoted to the post of headmaster. The teacher readily grabs the opportunity which turns out to be a complete night mare for him. He soon discover that he has no liking or aptitude for his new role, which demands completely different types of skills set, so his performance goes down in the new job, thereby affecting the future career. Sometime this may even lead to forced or early retirement also.

Neglecting fundamental constraint

Ignoring of critical limits such as mental and physical health often leads to more and more stress. This may leads to dependence on stress relieving substances from long hours and hard work -

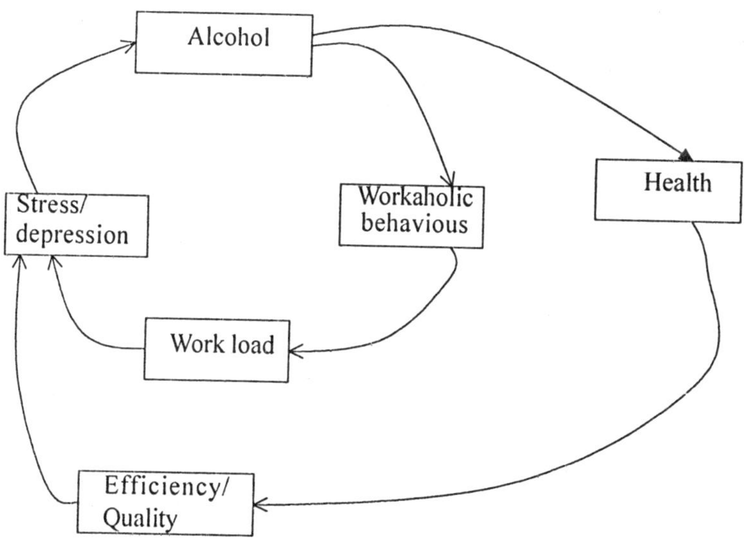

Fig 6.5. Neglecting Fundamental Constraint

such as alcohol/drugs/smoking etc. Too much consumption of these substances once again starts affecting health, which in turn affects work and thus the cycle continues to the detrimental effect for the individual. This is illustrated in Fig. 6.5.

Misplaced Priorities

Sometime there may be many such constraint and you may find it difficult to address them equally , so there is a temptation to tackle that one which is easy to handle but that constraint may not be the 'root cause" or the major constraint . So this often leads to misplaced priority which may often lead to compromise of long interests. Some time you may overlook a critical limitation of yours such as health, family needs, value/strengths etc for the sake of your growth. A very common example among working professionals is "please the boss", where an employee is able to get certain benefits and privileges as loyal subordinate but loose out by being a quality professional in his or her field. This is illustrated in Fig 6.6.

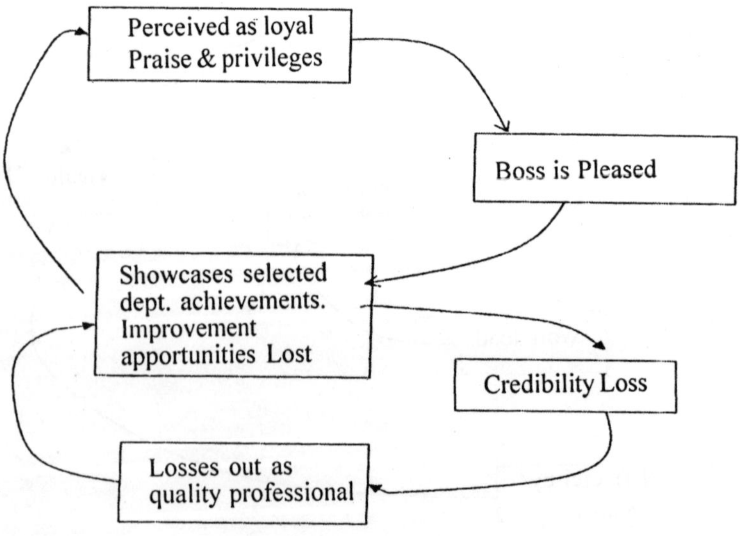

Fig 6.6 Misplaced Priorities

In the entire above illustrations one can observe two processes. One is a tangible and readily observable process which seem to occupy our attention easily and the other subtle, unobserved and latent process which remains hidden from our consciousness. This latent pattern does not surface immediately but takes time to grow and evolve, eventually constraining our progress and growth. For long term effectiveness, we need to identify such latent patterns and learn to minimize their negative effects on our career growth and development.

Factors that promotes identification of latent patterns and minimizing their negative effects

Listed below are some of the habits and competencies of successful professionals who are adept at minimizing the negative spiral of the latent patterns, while they are pursuing their vision and goals.

1. Ability to differentiate between short term goals and long term goals.
2. Tendency to see success and failure in totality. Ability to recognize the negative in success and even the positive in the failure.
3. Analyzing problems and situations from several perspectives- such as customer perspectives, stakeholder or management perspective etc.
4. A positive attitude for problem solving and learning from mistakes.
5. Keen sense of observation and keeping oneself updated on important developments.
6. Listening to others and Learning from feedback.
7. Being open to new ideas and experiments.
8. Networking with other professionals and learning from their experience.

You will notice that all the above factors represent either an approach of observing and thinking or certain skills or aptitude youfor solving problems for overall effectiveness. We now describe some typical latent patterns and their antidote. These are some examples and illustrations only; you can use a similar approach to examine many more situations and developing your unique antidotes.

Diagnosing typical latent pattern and their antidote
Symptom:

You had a dream growth for sometime but it has now declined or stopped. You feel as if you have hit a wall. A great amount of effort leads to a minimal improvement. It is causing frustration now.

Sub pattern	*Antidote*
Your erstwhile partnership working well for your growth has turned sour. There is no mutual trust.	While forming partner ship go step up by step .Trust comes as a result of mutually satisfying outcomes for both parties.
The people who were earlier supportive are no longer supportive.	The people supportive earlier may be jealous because of your higher success compared to them. Learn to down play your achievement and practice humility.
Too many people have started copying your ideas and they have spoiled the show.	Learn the art of strategic openness. Your best ideas may not be known to others. Keep learning and innovating. Practice creative thinking.
You have touched almost the pinnacle of your growth potential and hence improvement is bound to be slow.	Investigate your limits and critical constraints. Learn to relax. Seek ideas from people outside your profession. Move out into new areas.

(Contd.)

(Contd. Table)

Sub pattern	*Antidote*
There is a temptation to go for short term growth for immediate gain but this may compromise long term interest	Understand your GP and realign your short term priorities to your GP.
You tend to feel satisfied easily on account of past achievement and tend to bask in the past glory for too long. Soon you lose interest and enthusiasm.	There is lack of creative focus. Work along side people who like challenges and learn from them.

Symptom:

You are engaged in constant battle to maintain and fix things. But the problems keep coming back to you. Much of the time is

Sub pattern	*Antidote*
The solution works well for sometime but the problem keeps recurring. A lot of time is spent in dealing with it.	You mostly deal with the symptoms but do not try to find out the root cause of the problem. Collect systematic data and views of others who have faced similar problem in the past to find out the root cause of the problem.
Your solutions cause trouble for others and so there is opposition. Sometime the "mending" antagonizes your partners and well wishers.	Generate more alternate solutions and find out which is most acceptable to you as well as others. Try to involve those who are likely to be affected. If nothing else keep them informed.
There is a temptation to go for immediate fix for quick relief but this often leads to more trouble and cost.	Develop patience and wait for proper opportunity after collecting relevant information and expert advice from others.

(Contd.)

(Contd. Table)

Sub pattern	*Antidote*
You tend to feel satisfied by just dealing with problem and a temporary solution but the problem keeps recurring.	You have got habituated to a pattern of problem-relief cycle. Work out ways to prevent the problems in the first place.

spent in fire fighting there is hardly any time to plan for growth and advancement. It is causing frustration now.

Summarizing the Latent patterns in your career situation

Having diagnosed the latent patterns affecting your career and life, identify some typical patterns that are affecting your career prospects presently and work our appropriate strategies to deal with them.

1. What latent factors are affecting your career growth in terms of
   (a) Achieving new heights in career growth and advancement
   (b) Maintaining status qou in your present career and minimize disruptions
2. How do you would to make this pattern visible?
3. What strategies you can plan apart form the ones given in this chapter to remove bottlenecks?

7

Emerging Careers and New Opportunities

Introduction

To be truly successful in our area of interest or choice, we must always be aware of the emerging paradigm. A paradigm is nothing but a set of rules or assumptions, which govern the success in a given field. In a dynamic world the rules of the games keep changing all the time. All of us are familiar with the paradigm shift in our own life. To experience the effect of the paradigm shift just recall the time, when you joined college after completing your schooling. You might have experienced that many students who were very good in studies in school, suddenly became average performers in the new setting.

Similarly students, who were considered as laggard, became good students. This happens because of the shift in the paradigm. The paradigm of college studies is quite different from school. In the school there is lot of emphasis on discipline, lot of regular homework and constant feedback and guidance. However in the college, there is no such discipline and constant monitoring by the teacher. A student, who is dependent on teachers and thrives in regulated environment with constant monitoring and feedback, finds it difficult to make good use of the freedom and autonomy of college life.

Similarly for most of us our first job is a sort of paradigm shift. There is a joke about the first day of an IIM student in office, asking his secretary - so where is my first case? Obviously the student trained in the art of analyzing case studies looks at his job as –a series of case studies, which needs to be analyzed and solved. Many of us used to gaining success by applying certain approach, techniques or formulae during our student life tend to do the same when we take a up a job. If you are a student, it is important for you to understand that what ever you have learnt in your student days is going to be only partially useful for you even if you are in a technical field like software engineering or neuro-surgery.

The key difference is in the manner in which the problems or work situation come to you. In student life problems are presented to you in a structured manner and you are only concerned with the problem or specific aspect of the training in isolation. The classroom training is low context. The theories and practice seem to apply in the same way in all types of circumstances. However, the problems or issues in the work life are intricately connected to the work context. No problem comes to you in a structured manner. For e.g. when a patient comes to a doctor, he doesn't come with a particular problem of neuro-surgery. More often he may come with a bundle of problems-which may include blood pressure, sugar etc along with the problem which the specialist can handle as a neuro surgeon.

What ever you are studying right now, do not think that problems or issues will be presented to you in a structural way. In the student life your marks or grade improve by mastering the concepts and applying them to structured problems or applications. In work life your marks will improve based on your ability to apply techniques or solve unstructured problems of your customers (internal or external) in a flexible manner according to the need of the situation.

One simple way to understand the difference is to know that in your student life-theories and techniques are more important but in your professional life, the situation and its strategic analysis are more important than any theory.

Understanding business reality of your profession or Industry

Whatever your profession or whatever be the type of organization you work for, be it a large or small, public or private, profit or charity based organization, it is utmost important to know how your organization sustains itself in terms of revenue earning or funding or getting grants etc.

In any organization there are processes or jobs or activities, which are of critical importance for the financial health of the organization. Some of these activities may be important for a short-term perspective and some may be critical for a long-term perspective.

Just like knowledge and awareness of our deepest values and interest as envisaged in your Generic project (please refer chapter 2) are of critical importance for passion in your work and life in general, similarly the knowledge of the critical success factor of the industry or your profession is of equal importance in sustaining your passion and advantage in your career and profession life.

What ever job you are doing, you must know how your organization or business sustains itself, what is the critical success factors for your organization and in what way your job or role contributes to the success of the organization. There is a story of a receptionist, who started the practice of photographing important customers (alongside company logo) at the time of their arrival to the reception Desk. When asked how this idea came to her, she said that sending this photograph to our customer with our company logo in the background help us in connecting emotionally to the customer. This also reminds him of his visit. It can possibly lead to a work order. This small example shows that it is always possible to connect to the strategic purpose of the organization irrespective of your position or role.

Emerging Careers and career metamorphosis

More often you will see that it is the developments on several fronts such as technological, social, consumerisms, judicial activism, govt policy etc that leads to the demand for new or specialized types of product or services. New career opportunities are created since the need is not adequately addressed in a satisfactory manner or there is a looming threat of jeopardizing the interest of markets, consumers or society at large.

By being aware of these trends you can shape your career according to the changing demands of the society. This way you also contribute to the society as well find more meaning to the work you do. If you are bored in your present career and wish to change your career, it will be useful for you to keep a track of the changes that are taking place in the world of work and career. Even if you like your career and enjoy your job, it is still possible that your field may undergo a transformation and that you may find that your job, skills etc have become totally outdated in view of the new developments.

Let me illustrate this with an example. In the beginning of nineteenth century there were carriage companies in Europe employing hundreds of thousands of employees in the road transport business. However with the advent of Motor vehicles, many of these companies and the jobs they were providing were wiped out. Many employees lost their bread and butter. But those who were enterprising and were watching these changes carefully were well prepared. These employees took time off to learn the new skill and were ready to hit the road as soon as the next job opportunities came in. In fact since this was a new field and many people were not available, they could make the most of the situation. It is also possible that as a result of such changes, a new career opportunity may arise in an area of your interest or even hobby

All the areas of economy and business are interrelated. Innovation in one area may impact developments in many other areas. However we as individuals can make some understanding of these changes by applying our mind to it in a creative manner. So what would be the key developments in my career field of interest is not an isolated question, because development in other fields could also be affecting your field. It is stressful to make predictions about the future. Millions of ideas emerge every day. Only a few make their day. Some are too early for their time. Many simply die out for lack of marketing and some ridiculed ones emerge as winner. However all this complexity should not deter a good thinker to set about the task of thinking and making some possible predictions about "What is coming" on the basis of reasonable assumptions, emerging trends and the facts surrounding his career field.

An extremely useful way to look for new developments that could be supportive to your career growth is to be in touch with the changing requirements of diverse user groups or customers. The perceived boundaries of your profession must not deter you in asking the question such as –Whether my professional skills may meet the requirements of other users/customers/ industries/ groups apart from what I serve presently?

As a result of developments in the various fields, new career opportunities hitherto unknown are emerging. The developments in diverse areas as technologies, social, political, economical and so on can have an impact on the existing career as well as future career opportunities. Usually, the first one to see such possibility is the people who are in direct touch with the markets and changing customer's requirements. How such knowledge has lead to career metamorphosis for several people is illustrated next.

A Hobby converted to a satisfying career

A few days back I came across a professional who called herself a dance therapist. I found her profession very unusual and told her so. While talking to her I learnt that she home maker, dancing was her hobby and she used to train children in dancing just for her own interest. It was more out of fun and there was hardly any earning in it. She told me she came across the term "dance therapist" two years ago in a women's magazine. She searched the Internet and did some research on it. She associated herself with an HR trainer who was living in the same locality and

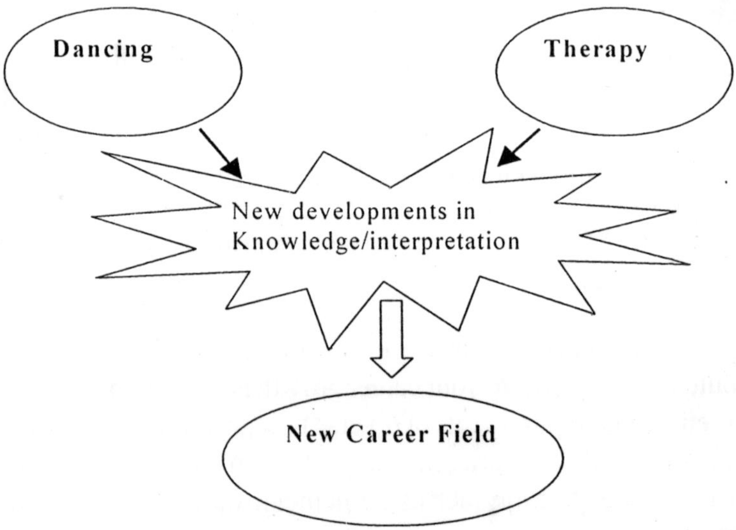

Fig. 7.1

thus got her first training session in a corporate training program on "Work life Balance". She told me she is really enjoying her new career a lot because –"I was always interested in a career, which improves the health of people, as well as allows me to persue my passion". So now she has found a career, which gives her the opportunity to do both while earning decent money.

This is shown in the diagram below.

A police officer shifts to a satisfying career with an NGO

Many of us are familiar with how Kiran Bedi, a police officer was shunted to IG prisons due to political reasons. However instead of getting demoralized by this she used her new posting to revive her interest in reforming the prisoners and serving the disadvantaged people. Her reformation efforts through vipasana are now well known to all of us through media. This experience of working for the helpless and downtrodden eventually gave her the right kind of experience for a second innings of a successful career with NGO's.

An Army officer shifts to corporate World

An officer dissatisfied with his career uses his posting in a peace station for pursuing a part time MBA and then shifts to corporate world as a successful HRD professional.

An IAS officer shifts to corporate World

An IAS officer frustrated due to frequent transfer and political interference in his work, finds one posting in the Public Sector of some interest to him. He uses his time well to understand the industry, develops right contacts and makes a move to private sector eventually enjoying a great second innings in the corporate world.

A math's teacher in banking Industry

A young math teacher comes in contact with some finance professionals and soon realizes that his mathematical abilities have great demand in an emerging field known as actuarial science. Earlier he thought that the only user of his skills were his students. He eventually finds a good break in a foreign bank and his career is completely metamorphosed.

A storekeeper in retail sector

A store keeper cum salesman in a military canteen learns about the boom in retail sector. He takes up a short time evening course in retail management, gets his first break as showroom in charge and transforms his career to fast track.

A Tutor who charges in dollars

An excellent English teacher comes to know through a consultant about the possibility of tutoring foreign students over the net and transforms her low paying career to a very high paying one where she gets paid in dollars.

An anthropologist in participatory Research

A young lady contends with sociology in graduation because she couldn't get admission in her favourite stream of economics. However she does much better than her own expectations when she finds a good opportunity in participatory research in a foreign development agency.

A Banking professional shifts to a career as Computer Security Auditor

A banking IT professional is trained in Computer Security Audit by his company and finds this as emerging career field with extremely promising prospects. Sometime back no one had heard of a full-fledged career in the field of computer security auditing. Though computer security was always important but computer professionals particularly those dealing with networks etc were dealing with it. Auditing was always thought to be something relates to accounting, but today you have firms which are specializing on auditing of systems security. If you look at the evolution of this as a career field, you will see that this has happened due to the increasing number of highly sophisticated cyber crimes. So with the growing incidences of cyber crimes by techies it has become important to go for a specialized branch to deal with this issue. More so in many countries it has become mandatory to have an independent party do the auditing so as to protect the interest of the consumers.

HR guy to a SAP Professional

Shekhar an HR guy was stuck and frustrated by lack of career opportunities in his present job. He comes in contact with consultants from E & Y who were helping in designing the new PMS for the organization. It is at that time that the idea of taking up career as a consultant which could be more rewarding as well as interesting came to him. From the consultants he learns about the emerging career opportunities in ERP consultancy for functional specialists. He takes up a short term course in HR SAP and transforms his career into a highly lucrative field.

New Career Opportunities

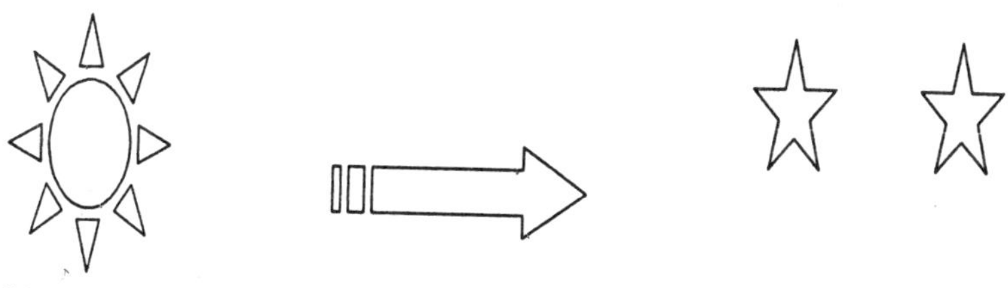

Shekhar's Positive Core

- Aptitude and willingness to learn new techniques
- Has good exposure to HR practices & system in a best employer company

Working knowledge of computer and process concepts

New Career Opportunities

- SAP as emerging area of opportunity.
- Opportunity to learn Global best practices

Fig 7.2

Viewing your career interest in a flexible manner

When you look at your career interest from the perspective of your GP, it becomes easy for you to look at it in a flexible manner so as that you are open to all possible opportunities that are emerging in and around your area of interest. The diagram below shows how your area of interest may have many more applications beyond what you are familiar with presently.

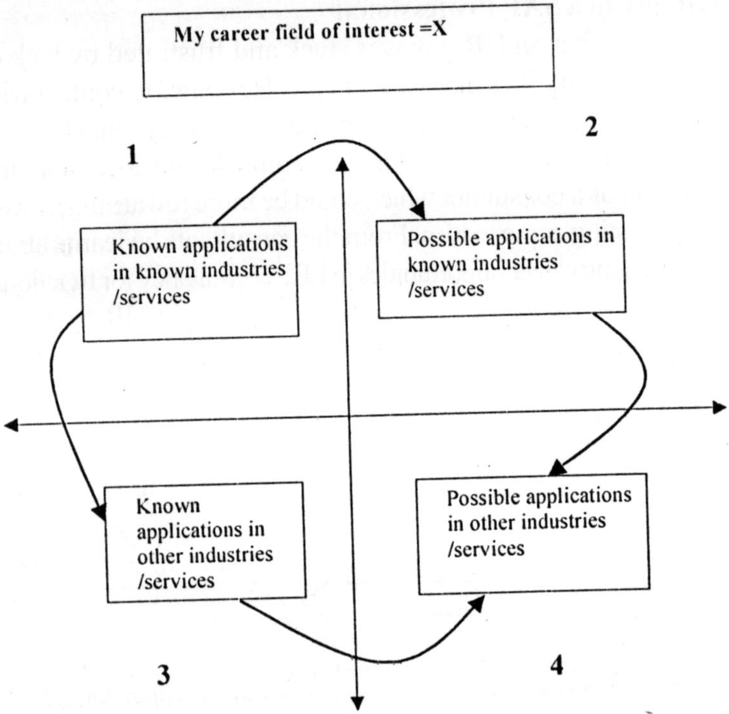

Fig 7.3

Let me illustrate an example of a creative decision by a person. A friend of mine was desperate to change his career to a different industry in which his experience was negligible. He was a civil engineer with about 3 years of experience in construction of residential complexes. He was keen to join an organization that was into design and Construction of airports.

It had many a lucrative projects for Airport expansion, city side developments, design of intelligent buildings, airport terminals etc. The evening before he was going for the interview he considered his strengths and weaknesses and discussed these with his colleagues. His colleagues suggested many things. But basically there advice was all the same in one way or the other. To emphasize that he is a team player, has exposure to projects which could be considered similar to airports design and construction, and that he is a great learner.

In the evening he thought over all these choices and realized that there is nothing greatly appealing about these, because the employer was looking for people with experience in airport. So he decided a novel approach based on his unique strength (GP). While emphasizing all his strengths, he candidly admitted at the interview that he had hardly any knowledge or experience about airports.

The interviewer was amazed and asked him –Why did you apply for this and he said. "Sir –I am not here to contribute to your organizations in what it is already strong. I am here to contribute that which is my unique strength and that is – project management skills, since your advert says that you want results. Then he reeled out his achievements relating to timely completion of projects and savings achieved by him. The interviewer was astonished at his depth of knowledge and he got the job.

The above example once again demonstrates the fact that a person who is knowledgeable about the customer or user requirement may be a valuable asset to an industry, even though he may not have any previous background or knowledge in that industry. This may partly be because such a person would not be biased or prejudiced (or overly concerned about the norms and practices of that industry) and so may be an extremely useful source of new ideas and innovative practices. A key question which we all need to ask ourselves is –What are those transferable skills which can be useful in solving key problems of users or satisfying the requirements of key stakeholders and customers in a better way.

Transferable skills and new skills

While looking for new and exciting career possibilities, you would invariably find that there are some skills from your existing repertoire of skills that can be easily transferable to a new area or field. These can be termed as transferable skills and may have diverse applications in a variety of situations. However apart from these there may also be other skills that you need to add for finding a good career break and which may lead to a higher possibility of career growth. We must be open to learning additional skills, when we realize that there are certain aspects of a field of interest about which we are unfamiliar. Even here there are two ways in which you can learn additional skills. One is of course through the formal means such as doing a professional course, the other is learning through informal sources. For working professionals the informal learning can be particularly useful, because often they may not be able to find time for a full fledged course. Apart from this many a time it is not really easy to find a professional course which really suits your requirements. In such a scenario learning through informal sources is a good idea and may often precede learning through a formal course, if that is a formal requirement for a particular job position.

Learning through Strategic Thinking

Have you ever experienced a crisis situation in your business or organization or even your home? If yes, have you noticed that there are certain people who are invariably consulted at the time of crisis, irrespective of their position or rank in the organization? These are the people who have made their reputation as leaders. Such people soon become part of the expert group in the organization and are involved in important decisions on most occasions. How does it happen? Have you ever wondered what the characteristics of such people are? More than any thing else such people are strategic thinkers. They have an ability to think strategically, in a calm and stress free manner and are able to focus their attention to real and critical issues rather than being carried over by emotional reactions to the situation.

Strategy is a term, which is more commonly used in the corporate world. However strategic thinking is needed in every sphere of life. Many a time problems, trends, needs, events or situation in our personal or professional life appear to constitute a undivided whole or seems to be a packaged black box. However a good thinker does not accept things on their face value but goes deeper by dissecting the issues or problems into specific constituent parts. The ability to break a bigger problem into small constituents or parts and analyzing them often leads to rediscovery of the significance and interrelationships of the various constituents. Like a jigsaw puzzle all these constituents are then reassembled in a way that will maximize the overall advantage.

The forte of a strategic thinker is the ability to learn from diverse people and their experiences. This enables the flexibility of thinking to come up with realistic responses to changing situations. When facing a tough situation, it is often vital to formulate the key questions about the situation in different manner so as to get a greater insight into the nature of the problem. The same thing applies to learning new skills or mastering situations that are not familiar to you.

There is a very important distinction between class room learning and real life learning. In real life no problem comes to you in a structured fashion. Your ability to learn and solve problems therefore greatly depends upon your ability to connect to the right kind of person or information- the person may be an expert, a vendor, suppliers or a colleagues of yours. The information may include knowledge of precedents, databases, previous reports, analytical tools etc. This ability to be connected to the right kind of persons and resources will not only help you solve different types of problems but also help in learning new skills that are relevant to your key users and stakeholders whom you wish to impress. So let us illustrate this with a few examples. Suppose you are working in the hotel industry and wish to impress your boss as well as customer by organizing a highly efficient and effective "Help Desk". So you wonder - where can I really get the best ideas about organizing this help desk? Now let us put this question in a different manner. So instead, let us ask – For which industry is this skill of organizing help desk extremely important? For what type of people such a skill could be a matter of life and death? When you ponder over this question for long, you will find that it is institutions such as Trauma centres or emergency services in reputed private sector that could be the answer for this. Since a small error in such services could have disastrous consequence, these institutions are likely to be extremely good in organizing an efficient and effective help desk. So you can learn about the best practices of organizing a help desk by visiting these institutions and talking to people there. It is highly unlikely that they would not cooperate, because you (from Hotel industry) are not a competitor for them.

If you are looking at new ways for improving customer service in your organization, it is not necessary that you would get the best ideas from the other organizations in the same industry. It is very much possible for you to get really bright ideas from organizations operating in other industries- particularly the industries where there have been a lot of competitive pressures. Highly competitive sectors such as telecom etc are presently excellent source of good ideas on customer services. This is because as they say- "Necessity is the mother of invention". Since organizations in happening sectors such as Telecom, banking etc are facing a lot of competitive pressures they are coming up with really good ideas to be a step ahead of each other.

Rowing in New Waters

When you plan for a career metamorphosis or even join a new job in a different industry or take a quantum jump such as from a middle level position to a top level position etc, you will invariably find that you do not have all the necessarily skills to thrive and excel in the new environment. However this must not deter you to take the plunge if that is really good for your career in long term. Of course what you would need is networking skills and the ability to learn from collaborating with experts and professionals from different fields. When you join a new organization it is very important to understand the expectations of those who hired you, peers and the team member that would work with you. It is important not to over commit, because failure to deliver what you commit could erode your credibility.

It is always a good idea to spend a considerable amount to time understanding the culture; always take elaborate notes so that you do not forget the important facts and information and spend time in listening to different people in the organization. Once you have understood the ground realities, take genuine initiatives such as Getting into the right task force, projects etc. Participatory activities such as these will ensure that you are in the visibility track, while also learning from the perspective of different people in the group. While taking new initiatives it will be more useful to dovetail your strength and expertise to the organizational priorities and expectations rather than the other way round.

In our life there will always be times when you should be aspiring to set for yourself ideal professional or career goals. There would also be a time when you need to avoid the worst. The habit of strategic thinking helps us to break out of the "patterns" that entraps us in predetermined and predictable responses. One good test is to ask your wife or friend to try to predict your response to a given situation and if they can always do that, then consider that you have been entrapped into a pattern of response.

Success in career and job needs to be summoned by creating alternatives and careful planning, it can never come unplanned. It must be backed by daily use of imagination and constant training in logical thought process. It is not that you apply strategic thinking only when confronted with unexpected problems or obstacles, but we must adopt the practice of strategic thinking as a matter of habit. If you want to progress in this art, you should approach strategic thinking with real enthusiasm in the same way some people get into solving logical problems such as suduko, or any stimulating mental exercise of your choice.

This has to be supported by Flexibility in thinking, which is about understanding the complete range of alternatives and constantly analyzing the cost-benefit of each one. True strategic thinker has a very strong sense of reality but can respond flexibly to the inevitable changes in situation. There is nothing like a perfect strategy. Strategy that is marginally superior under the given circumstances can lead to success. What is vital is of course timing and that is why execution is so important for successful implementation of any strategy.

How much initiative you take to update yourself on career aspects

The next 10 questions are aimed at assessing the extent to which you are taking initiatives on an ongoing basis to be aware of important issues relating to your job and career and keep track of important changes that are taking place in your field of interest in general.

Pl. answer the following questions as true and false.

(1) I scan through at least 3 professional journals in my professional area of interest every month

(2) I scan through at least 3 general magazines of personal interest every month.

(3) I spend about half an hour three times a week with professional friend or colleagues during lunch time/tea time etc exchanging latest information of mutual interest.

(4) I watch or listen to at least one TV /Radio program of my information

(5) I find time to interact with professional groups other than my work place through membership of professional body at least once a month.

(6) I read at least one good book of professional interest /career aspect once every two months.

(7) I travel at least twice a year for professional reasons.

(8) I usually regret that I could not get important information relating to my work place well in time.

(9) I am mostly unaware of the sources through which I can access any important information related to my career field of interest.

(10) I am able to get expert advice on important aspects through networking with professional friends/mentors/seniors etc.

If the answer to any of the above questions is "NO", there is a possibility to improve your awareness about career aspects. So, now list a few ideas about how to improve your change awareness quotient.

List ideas about how to improve your change awareness quotient

- Ideas about how to stay updated on important trends
- Ideas about how to explore the emerging fields of your interest
- Creative decision-making process. How to choose from among alternatives
- Case study in career metamorphosis and execution. Its analysis.

Being Columbus in finding new Career opportunities

It is estimated that new knowledge that is created in the last one decade is equivalent to that created in the preceding 50 years. The pace of change in every sphere of human activity is so fast that it is extremely difficult to keep track of it. There is so much happening in today's dynamic world that it is practically impossible to take account of all the developments that can have an impact on your career or work life. However though it may be difficult but there are great advantages in making a modest effort in that direction. Who knows your passion or interest may become a great career or business opportunity when things change.

The people who are well aware of the emerging opportunities are often the pioneers in a new field and hence they are able to reap a lot of benefits by taking timely steps. In fact if you look around yourself you will find a many great businesses are found on the principle of being the first one to make the most of a new opportunity. So to summarize we can say -

- There are careers which are comparatively new. When Columbus found America, he was the first one there. The early settlers who followed him were to make the most of the opportunity that the new land promised.

- Those who are the pioneers and early movers in any particular field are able to get the early bird advantage in a field that is promising.

- If the field is too new, there may not be too many jobs there at that particular time but at the same time there is not that much competition also.

- New career fields keep cropping up as a result of new technological developments, innovations, shift in socio-cultural aspects, change of Govt policies, political changes etc,changing values of the society etc. It is always advisable to keep a track of the latest developments that are taking place and make good use of the emerging opportunities.

- It is always possible that some of your skills will have useful applications in promising and emerging career fields. There is always a possibility to bridge the gap between your present qualification/profile and the desired profile through training, part time courses and networking with professionals provided you know where the gaps are.

8

The Reinforcing Cycle of Motivation

What happens to you when you get a project or task that is not interesting to you? You seem to find it a drag to carry on the task. Your enthusiasm goes down and you find that you are unable to give the desired attention and energy to it. On the contrary if the project or task is very interesting and meaningful for you, you keep returning to it whenever you find time. If you recall some of the instances of your life, you would invariably find some incidents of your life when you were highly enthusiastic about something.

Many children are very passionate about learning bicycle. For them it is like a great paradigm shift - from being able to walk and run to moving in by balancing themselves on two wheels. I am sure many would have experienced similar passion, while doing something the other at some stage in life.

When you are charged with this sort of passion, you trigger a reinforcing cycle of motivation, where each step in the motivation process leads to other steps in the reinforcing spiral of positive energy and passion as shown in the figure 8.1.

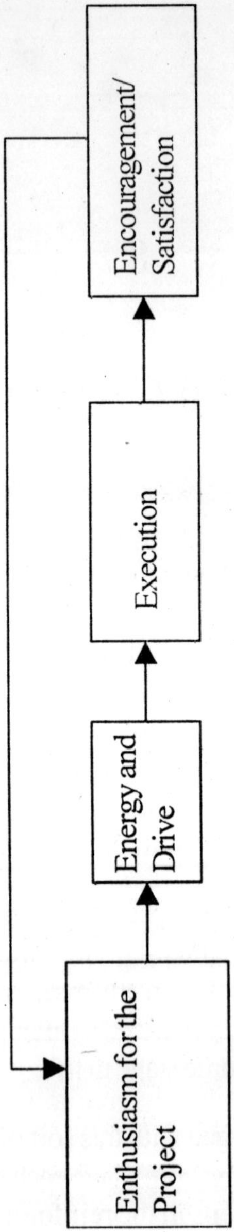

Fig. 8.1 Reinforcing Cycle of Motivation

Based on our learning from the chapter on Generic project, you would realize that in general, when the work or task is in accordance to our GP, it becomes easy to trigger the cycle of passion and on the contrary when the work and task is completely unconnected to our GP, it becomes difficult to generate the cycle of motivation and positive energy. We will return to this aspect shortly but now let us take a look at some examples which we often find in our work lives and which illustrates this point further.

Case example 1

A young HR trainee (a new joinee) was explaining it to me like this once. I am an extrovert and when I joined this company I thought that I would be working in a team, interacting with lots of people but to my disamay, none of this happened at least for the first 6 months. I was given a sort of project work which was mostly to be done on my own. I was put in HR Policy group and there was hardly any opportunity for interactions with other team members. I was on the verge of leaving the organization, when my mentor stepped in and redesigned my work for me in such a manner that the project started appearing quite interesting to me now.

Case example 2

A person, who abhors travelling, lands in a marketing job, finds the job very tough and so feels miserable. He was almost written off, till one day his boss discovers that he is very meticulous in record keeping and use of computer, so he redesigns his field job to a customer support executive who mainly interacts with customers via phones, handles querries and manages weekly MIS for the boss thus contributing substantially to customer satisfaction.

Case example 3

This is a case of a student who was good at science but didn't pay much attention to math. This student was passionate about science; he liked to study science and also carry out science projects but took little interest in math. His parent took him to a counselor. The counselor appreciated the student's interest in science but demonstrated to the student, how excellence in science is critically dependent on math by giving various examples from the lives of great scientists. The student was also shown the findings of a research project reported in the reputed Journal of Science. According to this research- **"Students who had more math courses in high school did better in all types of science once they got to college."**

Once the student was able to clearly see the link between science and math, he developed a similar interest in math also.

Learning from the Cases

In all the above cases we see that the mentor interpreted the role in a different manner so as to make the task more interesting and motivating. That is how each of them started finding their work interesting.

After going through the above cases you will realize there are certain aspects that lead to enthusiasm for work with respect to any particular situation, task or project etc. This is the first step to Motivation. The two factors which jointly influence the enthusiasm for work are as described below

- Inner core: Reflects the inherent preferences of a person. This normally comprises of his needs, aptitude and values.

- **Causal belief: is the subjective belief that successful completion of an act will lead to worthwhile outcomes.**

The significant difference in their energy or enthusiasm before and after the mentor or counselor stepped in can be analyzed under the two categories of "inner core" and causal belief. When these two aspects are positively associated with the task or a

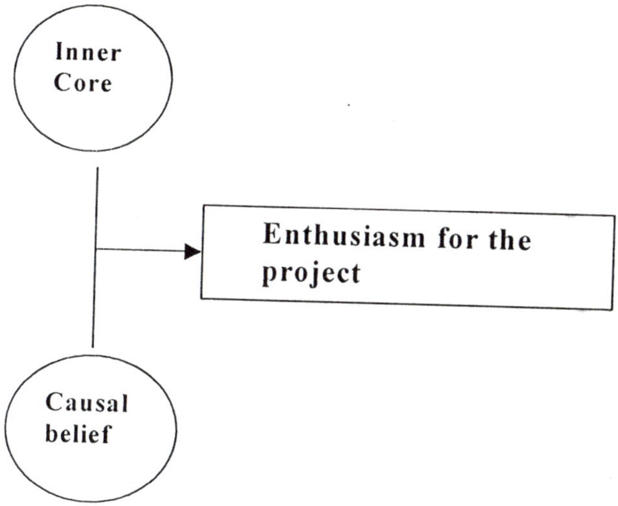

Fig. 8.2

given project there will be a significant increase in the enthusiasm and motivation of the person.

Inner Core

When the task at hand is in accordance to our nature and liking which also includes our values, needs and aptitude the mere fact of doing the task is its own reward. The task becomes something like our hobby. In the first case the young HR trainee being an extrovert initially found the task boring, however when her mentor emphasized that the project also means interviewing different executives and meeting them she started liking the same job.

In the 2nd case the marketing executive found the whole process of travelling and meeting clients abhorring, however when the nature of task was modified to contact customers over phone, keeping track of their requirement, providing feedback to colleagues and boss and also maintaining an MIS. The same task became quite interesting and meaningful to him.

Causal belief

Causal belief associated with a task denotes our subjective belief regarding the extent to which the given task or project will be useful in achieving our long-term goals. In layman's language it is something like a mental calculation – What will I get if I successfully complete the task. Will I get a promotion? Will my market Value improve? Will my CV become more prestigious? Will I gain contacts with significant persons etc? Needless to say causal belief associated with a task is both a question of what a person believes is important or his priority and subjective belief that the task at hand is in accordance to that priority in life.

In the third case the student interested in science was not taking his math seriously till the time the counselor explained to him how math was the basis of all scientific work. The counselor provided him interesting questions and exercises in science which required knowledge and skills of math. The student thus started finding math as useful, interesting and challenging due to his desire to excel in science. So the student realized that excelling in math will only help him to realize his long term aim of excelling in science and technology.

GP and Execution Excellence

One key Question that emerges from this is that how can we improve the Enthusiasm for work in a given situation like the one that is described in the case. Out of the two i.e Inner Core and Causal belief, it is easier to influence or change the Causal belief.. Inner Core typically depends on the personality –person's aptitude, liking, needs and what he values in life. This does not change in short term day-to-day situations.

However, causal belief is a belief about the importance of the task for the person's long-term goals and therefore this can be more easily modified by redesigning the task or interpretation of the task and its importance in such a manner so that the individual starts finding it meaningful. In all the above cases the subjects were lucky that they got an understanding boss/counselor or

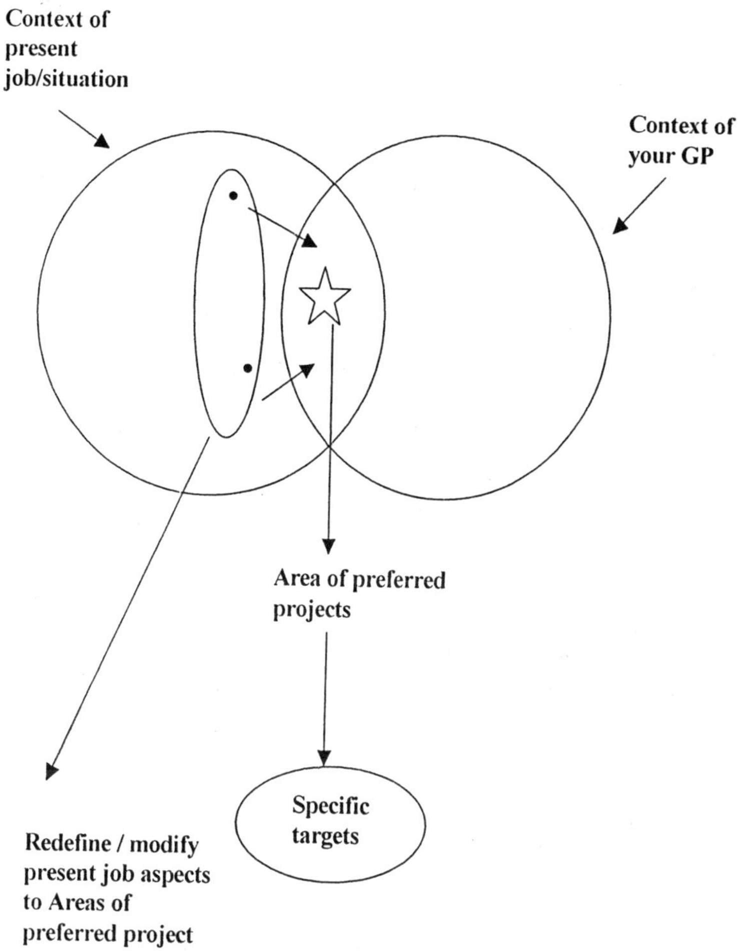

Fig. 8.3. Areas of Preferred Projects.

mentor who helped them in redesigning the task in a manner that the task became interesting to them. They started finding the task more meaningful. One has to bear in mind that we see things in different way and something, which is a problem to one may be an opportunity to another. The key is how you present and interpret the task to the person , so that he finds it meaningful in line with his own aspirations and interests.

The figure 8.3 shows the intersection of 2 sets, one comprising of tasks in the context of present job and second comprising of the context of your GP.The areas of preferred projects is the area of intersection between these two sets. When the and redefined to include long term interests, they become highly motivating and interesting to a person. As shown in the diagram above this process is useful for getting the most from your Generic project. When the targets are designed in the above manner, the specific goals become part of the broader vision as envisaged in the GP and hence are a strong source of motivation to the person.

Using the concept of Causal belief all tasks in your day to day work life are possible to be categorized in 4 possible ways as shown in the figure 8.4.

Quadrant 1: contains all the task/activities or projects that are important in your present job, which is expected by the boss but un important for your career growth according to you.

Quadrant 2: Contains all the task/activities or projects that are important in your present job as well as important for you from a long term perspective about your career growth.

Quadrant 3: Contains all the task/activities or projects that are unimportant in your present job as well as Unimportant for you from a long term perspective about your career growth.

Quadrant 4: Contains all the task/activities or projects that are unimportant in your present job but important for you from a long term perspective about your career growth.

	Unimportant for Long term goals	Important for Long term goals
Important for Present Goals	1	2
Un-important for Present Goals	3	4

Fig. 8.4. The Goal Grid.

In order to get the best out of our career and achieve our long term goals, we should try to operate from quadrant 2 as far as possible. We should take proactive interest and initiative to volunteer and /or negotiate to include such projects which essentially falls in quadrant 2. Similarly we must try to avoid all activities that fall in quadrant 3, since it has no value for us both in the short and the long run.

The main challenge for many people is how to deal with quadrant 1 activity. These usually contain the typical activities that are rewarding in the short run but are not of much value for giving you the best advantage for long term career growth and joy at work.

Sometimes you may find the activities that are quadrant 1 for you are quadrant 2 for somebody else. This means that these activities which are not very significant for you could be important for somebody else and vice versa. Therefore it may be possible to create a win-win situation for both you and your colleagues by making arrangements to exchange some of your responsibilities and tasks with each other.

The best way to ensure that you get the most out of your day to day activities is to take a proactive approach towards taking responsibilities by the cooperation of members of your team, colleagues as well as the boss. Sometime it may also be possible that the by redesigning a task in a different manner you would start finding it more meaningful both from the context of your present job and also from the long term perspective of your generic project. The tasks of the quadrant 1 are the most suitable candidates for redesigning.

Sometimes the task or activity may undergo a complete metamorphosis by breaking it into different elements and then combing them in such a manner that the nature of task and its attractive ness changes completely. Sometimes you will be surprised to see that by dropping a few elements of a responsibility and adding one or two activities or changing the approach or methodology of the very task which is meaningless for you makes it appear very interesting.

A creative thinker uses an approach by which the different elements of the responsibility or task are combined in such a manner that the task undergoes a complete metamorphosis.

This approach of combining various elements of the task is illustrated in the diagram below.

The first column in the above diagram illustrates the way most people operate by scheduling different activities according to the pressing requirements of the present situations. Each task is seen as inflexible steel balls- a series of independent tasks, the elements of which can not be combined in any other manner. In the next column, tasks are seen as rubber balls, which mean unimportant elements of the tasks are squeezed to deal with the most important priorities only. In the last column tasks and activities are seen as clay balls, which mean that each task or activity can be creatively redesigned by combining elements of individual tasks. In this process the tasks are completely redesigned to suit the present job as well as long term goals.

This approach of viewing your task and responsibilities as flexible clay ball is helpful, when you find that parts of job are not aligned to your GP. So, if you find your job boring or thankless, while not contributing much to your career, try breaking the job into small parts or tasks. Play with these parts, as children play with clay and then recombine these different parts in a creative manner. Add some interesting colours to give your job a new meaning for yourself as well as the organization you work for.

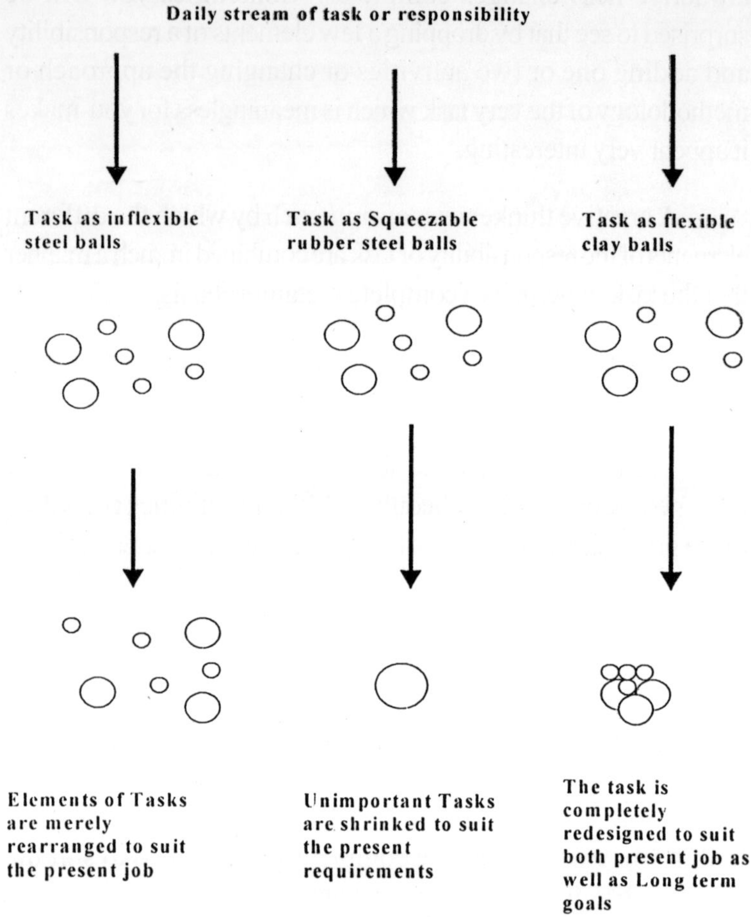

Fig. 8.5. Interpreting Tasks, responsibilities and situations

Aligning daily stream of activities with Long term goals

The diagram above illustrates that the daily stream of activities is like independent tasks that we need to carry out as part of our job or responsibilities etc. It's like all that we do or go through in a day's work. These independent activities could be very monotonous or boring when seen in isolation, however they become a harmonious whole when they are seen through the framework of our generic Project. It is then possible to examine each activity or task in relation to its contribution to our Generic project and thereby to our long term aims. When seen in this light every activity becomes part of a zig saw puzzle leading us closer to the solution. It reduces the dichotomy between what we are doing presently and what we wish to aspire for. It reduces the need to compartmentalization life into different segments-the home life, the office life, the work, the hobby etc. There is an integrating framework which helps us in integrating all our plans and initiatives whether in home or office.

When the daily activities/tasks or responsibilities are examined with the framework of our generic project it helps us in giving a creative response to our situation. The elements of the tasks or responsibilities are creatively combined and redesigned

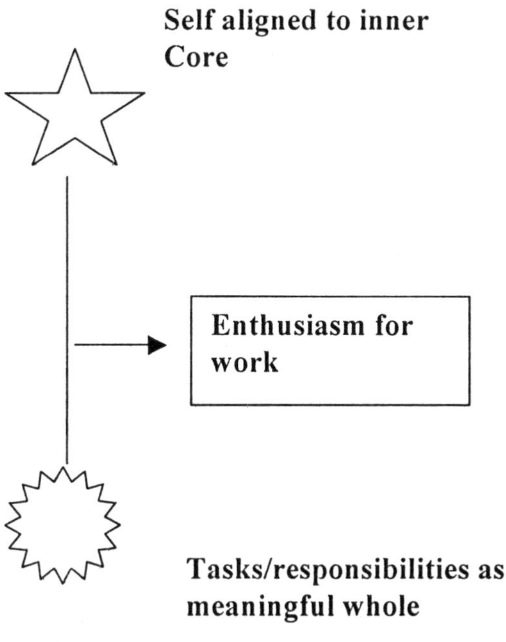

Fig. 8.6.

in a manner to suit our long term interests and aspirations. The thought process involved in this is shown in the diagram on the previous page.

This process of looking at each piece of initiative as part of Long term strategy helps you in aligning your present situation with both your inner core (inner strengths-Values, needs and aptitude) and your long term aims. The process thus leads to a strong passion or desire to excel in your area of interest, which has continuity with your present context also and which is not merely a dream regarding something for which initiative would be possible in future only. Of course if your present job or context does not provide enough opportunity or flexibility you would try to move to a different job or context (this may include internal transfer also). Again the above process will help you in deciding what context or job will be suitable in kindling this passion to perform. This is based on the strength of your inner core and Possible opportunities which transform the present work into what is meaning full for you in the long run.

Integrating goals with spontaneous nature of our work life

Setting specific goals and Planning are certainly important in life. However our ability to execute our plans greatly depend on how we integrate the goals and planning aspect with spontaneous nature of our work context including various situations we encounter in our daily life. So we now turn our attention to developing excellence in execution of what you had planned as specific target and what just happened to come your way in your day-to-day life.

If you observe yourself every day for a period of time, you will observe that your work or activity pattern has two main aspects. Firstly there are those aspects of your work, which you specifically plan to achieve during the course of the day or week or month etc. Secondly there are those aspects of work context or daily situations, which just come to you without asking your preference one way or the other. These are people, situations, tasks or information, which just come to you during the course of the day. Sometimes you may not like these unplanned intrusions in your life and may like to avoid any involvement.

However, you may still end up spending time even to avoid any involvement with such situations. There are times when you are not clear whether an intrusion is unwanted or not, in the first place and then there are also times when you may not be sure whether an unwanted intrusion is avoidable or not and if at all avoidable at what cost.

Often you will find that these two aspects are intertwined in such a way that it is difficult to separate one from another. Often one leads to another. You bump into somebody you were avoiding. However while talking to him you are able to sniff something significant. You check your sources and derive important information, which helps you in avoiding some pitfalls while working on one of your favorite projects. So whenever you find yourself disenchanted with your present job responsibilities, think of possibilities that you may not be aware of by using this Questionnaire.

This questionnaire will help you in being aware of possibilities arising in your present job or work situation.

Questionnaire: Assessing linkage of present tasks or projects to your Generic Project

1. Whether the task or its context (TC) provides an opportunity to interact with a resource group such as top mgmt, experts related to my GP, important information, databases, customer etc that can facilitate my GP?

2. Are there past success cases of individuals (those who got benefited in their career) who were associated with this TC previously?

3. Is it possible for me to get an informal feedback on this TC from past success cases as well as those, which were not?

4. Will the involvement lead to some tangible benefits-such as a trade certificate, license to do something, possible business association for self, critical information etc, know how of a particular aspect?

5. Does it fullfill a particular personal need ignoring which right now can have some consequences thus indirectly affecting my GP?

6. Are some inputs for you dependent on some key people working in this TC?

7. Are some places to be visited in this TC of particular importance to you?

8. Does it lead to improving efficiency on some related aspects, which will free more time for my GP in future?

9. Does it lead to some technology or resources like software etc that can facilitate my GP in future?

10. What are the costs involved in this TC in terms of time, energy, money etc

The enthusiasm for work of course is the first step to motivation, so now let us see how this enthusiasm for work can be converted into systematic effort for achieving our objectives.

The next step: Enthusiasm to Systematic effort

The enthusiasm for one's work does not mean that the person would put in the desired effort for achieving his cherished goals. Can you recall some of your own cherished goals /activities which you resolved to carry out with great enthusiasm? Does it sound familiar? The New Year resolution or any decision that you vowed to carry out soon petering out in the maze of other priorities and contingencies and a time comes when we simply forget the promise that we made to our self.

I would like to encourage you to discuss this apparent paradox- the situation where though you have great interest or enthusiasm for something but now seem to be slightly laid back, unsure of yourself despite your initial enthusiasm. The diagram below shows that enthusiasm for work leads to effort only when there is positive sense of confidence regarding the task or project at hand.

The apparent paradox can be explained by pointing out that the enthusiasm for work is not sufficient for making a person put effort on a project or task. The enthusiasm for work interacts with the "sense of self confidence" to produce the first observable step towards taking some action or putting effort. This sense of self confidence is the set of belief regarding the link between making an effort and actually performing well.

So, how do we improve our sense of self confidenc? The first step to improve the sense of confidence is to set meaningful targets that are moderately tough. We should not set for our self targets that are impossible to achieve, at the same time we should not set such targets that are so easy that they do not challenges us sufficiently. The psychology of setting to high or too low a target is the same. We wish to avoid failure rather than approach the challenge with an open mind.

Figure 8.7 shows that enthusiasm for work leads to effort only when there is positive sense of confidence regarding the task or project at hand.

It is something like this- that our mind gives a subtle message- that the idea is good, the goal is important but somehow I am not too sure whether I will be able to make it (i.e. there will not be

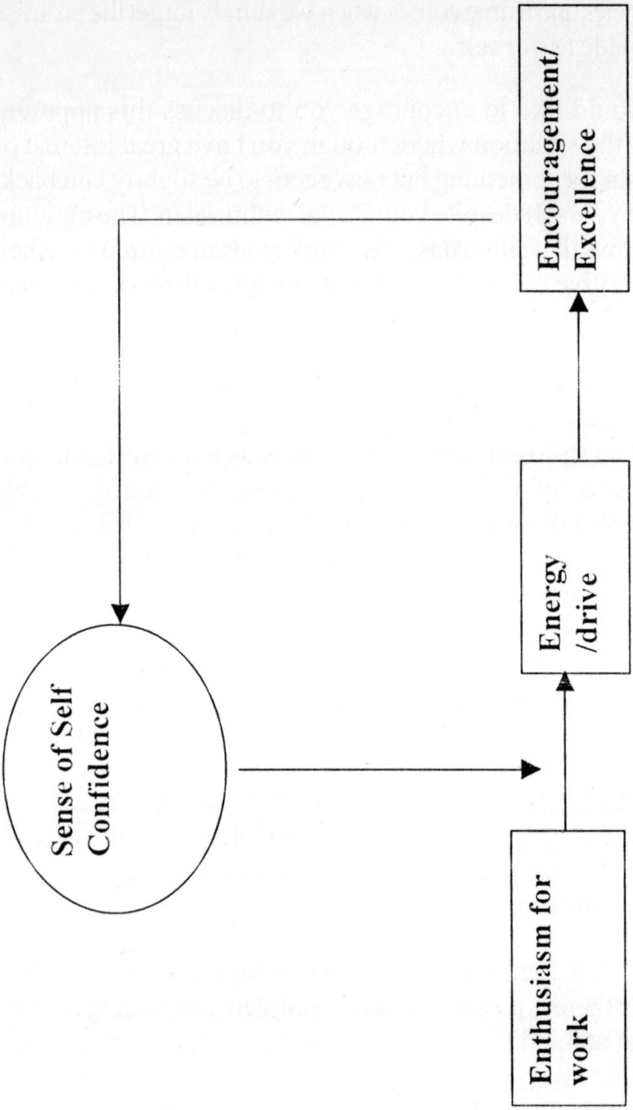

Fig. 8.7. Self Confidence and the Drive to Perform.

enough time, resources, it will be too difficult etc.). When we keep making such promises to our self and then break them conveniently our sense of confidence further declines. Every time we make a new promise, our unconscious mind tells us –it will not work this time also and hence we get caught in the negative spiral of overpowering disbelief and doubt.

So, how do we improve our sense of self confidence? The first step to improve the sense of confidence is to set meaningful targets that are moderately tough. We should not set for our self targets that are impossible to achieve, at the same time we should not set those targets that are so easy that they do not challenge us sufficiently. The psychology of setting too high or too low a target is the same. We wish to avoid failure and approach success with an open mind.

If we have a bigger target it is very important to divide it into manageable chunks so that we get a feeling of control over the target. I remember an instance when I started my career in the 90's. At the end of the year I was filling my performance appraisal form. I saw two columns – Left hand, for mentioning the targets that were set in the beginning of the year and right hand for what was achieved. I was filling the form for the first time. I was clear about what I had achieved but I had no clue as to what were the targets set for me in the beginning of the year. So I went to my boss and asked about it. My boss gave me a sympathetic look and said "See you are filling this form for the first time and that is why this doubt. It is very simple first be clear of what you have achieved and then write the same thing as your target in the left hand column."

Unfortunately many of us go through our personal achievement cycle in the same way. This is something like saying first hit the arrow wherever you ean and then make a bull's eye where your arrow struck. It is very important to define your target clearly. In case it is a larger target you may divide it into small chucks so that you have a clear sense of direction, while you set about in your journey. It is like continuously asking yourself–what will I see, what will I hear and what will I feel during various parts of my journey that will tell me that I am proceeding in the right manner and direction. See those pictures very clearly–vivid and full of colors and they will become inspiring milestones in your long journey towards your goal.

Setting specific targets does not mean that these have to be inflexible. You can constantly review the targets to take into account the changes in your environment but what is definitely important is that these should be somewhat stressful targets – neither too easy nor extremely difficult and you must constantly raise the bar in front of you.

It has to be pointed out that the "sense of self confidence" is shaped both by our initial assumption and belief about our self and the situation, as well as our past experience with respect to the situation or task at hand. It is said that people who are positive in their attitude and optimistic tend to believe that they can measure upto any given problem or situation and hence have a high sense of "self confidence" with respect to most tasks or project that they embark on.

As shown in fig 8.8 the past experience of dealing with similar problems or situations is likely to boost the "sense of self confidence". However, the person with high belief about himself and his abilities may also have a high "sense of self confidence" in general on his ability to take up various and diverse problems. Basically it is like a self-reinforcing cycle. Initial belief- making a person take up challenges and the success in turn helps to reinforce the initial belief further.

The final steps for execution excellence

Once you have started a process of systematic effort towards your cherished goal, the two key factors that need to be looked at at this stage are defined below.

- Competence- is the knowledge, skill, attitudes and moral capabilities an individual brings to a situation.

- Execution strategy – is the approach an individual develops to go about what they are supposed to be accomplishing and how.

The above model shows that the Raw material of Energy and drive can only be converted into execution when the person has the required competence as well as proper strategy of execution. There are various types of competencies that may be required for being able to complete the different projects satisfactorily. Execution strategy precedes the competences and the resource requirements. When we know what exactly we need to do, including what method or approach we are going to take i.e we have the accuracy of role perception it will also be possible to know what type of competencies we need for fulfilling the requirement of the role. We can also plan to generate the necessary resources and capabilities that may be required for accomplishing our goals.

Let me illustrate this with an example. A lady once told me this story about learning to drive. She wanted to learn driving as it was very important for her and would have given her a lot of flexibility to commute to office and home as per her requirement without depending on the chartered bus. She told me that despite all earnestness she couldn't develop the confidence and has now given up. So I asked her how she had started to learn it. She told me that she enrolled in a driving school and then started learning in the open ground one hour every morning and continued like this for about 10 days.

After 10 days she was quite confident that she had mastered the art. However the next day when she started driving on the road she felt extremely nervous. The traffic was coming from all

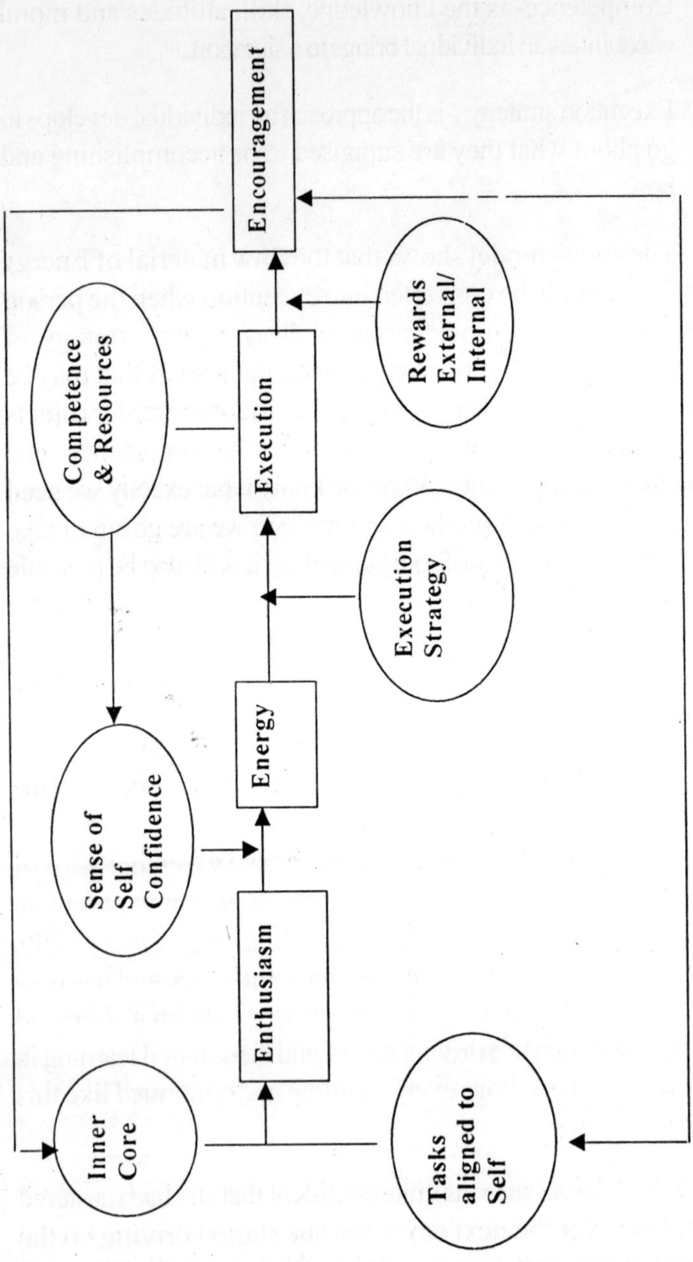

Fig. 8.8. Integrated Approach for Execution Excellence.

sides and it was difficult to judge. Suddenly in her nervousness she hit a cyclist. The cyclist was not hurt but created a scene and demanded money for damaging his cycle. On knowing this her husband asked her to stop driving as he felt "she didn't have the aptitude for it.

Thus it can be seen that the lady couldn't master the skills because her learning method or training was wrong. In actual she should have practiced 2 days on the open ground, another 2 in the colony early in the morning and their taken the final plunge onto the nearest main road.

What you see here is an example of failure due to lack of proper execution. The same thing holds good for anything which you wish to achieve whether it is learning to drive a car or driving your career. Unless you plan your execution strategy, which means working out the details of what, where, how and when; it would

Fig. 8.9. The process is shown in Fig 8.9.

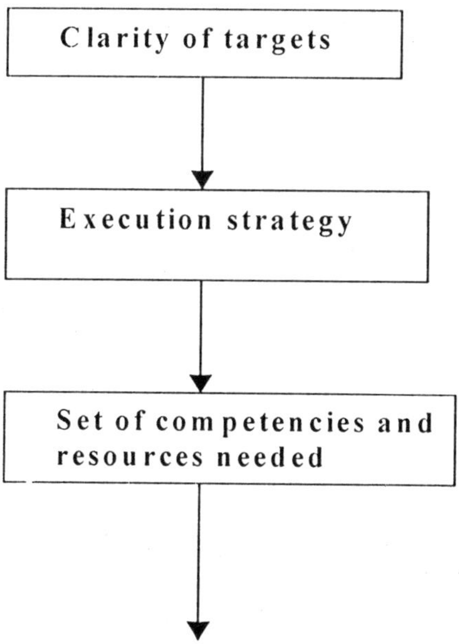

be difficult to develop the required competence and generate the necessary resources to achieve your goals.

Example of competencies required for a job requiring excellent customer relations and hospitality skills.

Competencies	*Present level*	*Desired level*	*Action Plan to bridge the gap*
Job knowledge	1	2	
Communication	2	2	
Human Relations	2	3	
Organizing & Implementation skills	2	4	

- Level 1: Unfamiliar
- Level 2: Familiar
- Level 3: Practiced
- Level 4: Expert

In the same way it is also possible to make a similar table for identifying the resources that you will need and action plan to bridge the gap between what you have and what you would require. The cycle is complete when there is a reward for a specific achievement of yours. All rewards may not be in your own hand. However when you have aligned yourself to something that is of long term importance to you and you continue to build expertise or learning in that field, acquiring of that expertise or learning is a reward in itself.

Of course it is much more of morale boosting, when you get external recognition for what you have achieved, which further reinforces your interest and enthusiasm in the work. Even if immediate reward is not there do not think that your performance and the confidence that you built in your abilities will go waste. If your present boss or colleagues do not recognize it do not worry because perhaps better opportunities are waiting for you and it will be only a matter of time when you will be ready to get your next important career break.

Let us recap the 4 steps that we need to master in the art of execution.

1. Aligning present tasks/activities/context to meaningful Long term Goals
2. Setting specific Challenging goals
3. Work out execution strategy to achieve the goals.
4. Work out competency and resource requirements to execute the strategy

9

Branding for success

In the movie world actors and actresses get branded according to their personality, specific strengths and characteristics. For e.g. an actor is branded as action hero, another may be branded as character artist, still another may be referred to as comedian etc.

Once an actor performs a role and does well in it, people start identifying him or her with that role, so he gets more of the similar stuff and thus gets branded as a particular type. Of course there are actors like Naseeruddin shah, Amitabh Bacchan etc for whom, it is very difficult to say whether they are of one type or the other. This is because over the period of time they have done all sorts of role and it is very difficult to say whether they are this or that. However if you recall there early days you would realize that even these people started there career as particular type- Amitabh as action hero and Naseer as Character artist.

A similar thing happens when you pursue a career or job. You get branded as finance man, HR person or marketing guy and so on. There is a particular image associated with each of these careers. Some time it can be a sort of stereotyping by people. For e.g. Finance people are very serious. I once met a senior HR person who after rejecting a candidate for a position of finance executive, remarked- Can't be a real finance guy, I am yet to see a real finance guy who talks so much. Though such stereotyping may not be logical, but unfortunately a large section of our society is influenced by these images or thoughts.

All brands whether associated with a product or service, employer or career field are associated with a particular image about it. Brands are always associated with images. For e.g when you think coca-cola you get an image of the life style and type of people who often consume this drink. Similarly when someone is introduced to you as an ex-IIT, you perceive that person to be highly intelligent, scholastic and so forth. So let us look at some of the Brands and associated images relevant to career aspects.

Brand Type	*Some typical examples*
Institutions	IIT's, IIM's,Harvard,Doon school etc
Professional	Accounts, Merchant banker, IT, HR-Generalist, Advertising, Sales, Operations etc
Aptitude	People centric, quantitative, service oriented, process driven, outgoing, go-getter, aesthetic, nature lover etc
Organizations / associated work Culture	Best employer, A fun place to work, 24* 7 type, Bureaucratic, hierarchical etc
Lifestyle / Outlook	Conservative, traditional, religious, Jerk, modern, scientific, pragmatic etc

Some of these brand types seem to reinforce each other for example-IIT, modern, scientific. Similarly there could be brand types which could weaken each other. For e.g. IIT & superstitious etc. It is not necessary that all individuals who pass out from IIT will be scientific but that is how most people perceive the "image" of an IIT pass out.

The most important aspect of the branding process is that it helps us in creating an "Image' or favorable impression which opens some doors for us. However in our anxiety for creating a favorable Image on others, we often forget the importance of our own self Image. Self Image is the foundation on which we can create a strong favorable impression on others.

Self-Image

Each person holds an image about him/herself. This image is known as the person's self-image. The formation of self-image begins at the early childhood and continues till late teenage and even afterwards. A child forms the self-image based upon the early childhood experiences, interactions with the environment, schooling, and relationship with authority figures like parents, teachers, relatives and family members like siblings.

However, self-image is always an interpretation which a person makes of the data. This interpretation may be incorrect or correct. From the perspective of branding there are two key aspects of self image that we need to consider. One aspect is about factual data i.e the objective data relating to your past. This includes your credential such as–Any award, degrees, certificates, licenses, % of marks as well as aspects such as your family background etc.

The second aspect of data is more concerned about your future and this represent the subjective data which indicates your potential in terms of the context of new situation-which you are aspiring for. It is surprising to see that many people when they apply for a new position place a lot of importance on the first part but do not attach any importance to the second part at all.

If you see from the perspective of the future employer or customer etc you will find that what they are really interested is in your ability to deliver the result to their specific requirements and so they are interested on your past credential only to the extent that they are predictive of your future behaviour. One important source of predictive future behaviour is your motivations –"what are you working for", what kind of career you aspire for, what is the type of work which you will do with enthusiasm. Even if a person is highly qualified it may not mean that he will be great success in the job.

A majority of job positions particularly in the business world do not require the intelligence of an Einstein or a Newton. All they require is people who are sincere, willing to put in the hard work and achieve the results for themselves and the organization. In most of the situation what is basically required is a match between what the individual can achieve and requirements of the organizations. One of the best ways to explore this possibility of mutually satisfying relationship between employee and employer is by understanding the core strengths of the individual and how do they match with the job or organization requirements.

Benefits of aligning the Self-Image with your generic project (GP):

A person takes most of his/her decisions based upon the self-image he/she holds. Since the interpretation is usually done in the childhood, the interpretation may not be entirely true now in the current reality. Often people are not aware of the self-image they hold. When a person consciously tries to develop his self image to his natural strengths in accordance with his GP, the person appears to be natural and at ease with himself, when trying to project himself. This is because by doing this the person is creating his self-image, according to the natural potential he sees in himself.

On the contrary when you try to cultivate a self image which is totally away from your natural potential, you appear to be a fake. An HR professional once told me an interesting anecdote which illustrates this point. He told me that he once got a feedback from his colleagues that he is very soft with people and for being a successful HR professional he should be tough with people etc. So he started trying to create an image of being tough and started believing that he can be really tough with people. By projecting this self image along with other credentials he got a better job, where he was expected to be tough with people and retrench lots of people in a few months. A few months later he felt extremely miserable because obviously he felt that he has landed in a job which he is not enjoying at all. So he resigned from the job and changed career to a position which was more suitable to his real "self image" rather than his fake one. You may be successful in projecting yourself for short term. When you feign a Self image which is not natural to you; it would be difficult to maintain this image for long.

Imagine what you could be ...... and be it

So in nutshell we can say that for long term advantage the self-image should be cultivated around the key aspects of your generic Project –which represents your natural strengths with a pointer towards your future potential. To be more precise the self image must be cultivated around the following aspects:

- What is my inner core: What do I really like, what are my values, what is my aptitude and temperament, What is my core belief etc

- What are my abilities and resources

- What is my potential in relation to my unique strengths

Though your self image must always be built around your unique strengths, this doesn't mean that you should not be aware of your weakness. You should definitely be aware of the weakness so that you can work out arrangements like support from others etc so as to deal with them. This will help you in developing effective strategies and support systems to deal with those shortcomings which come in the way of your career aspirations. However, It is often more paying in life to further strengthen your strengths and project them rather than bothering too much about your weaknesses.

Branding Self – Meaning

- **Branding Self** is a process for creating a positive image and credibility about one's strengths and abilities to make positive contributions to organizations/ groups / customers / projects etc.

- It is the art and skill of presenting one-self in a natural way, conducting self with ease and elegance, without being perceived as arrogant, over bearish or trying to impress others.

- It facilitates initiative and assertiveness based on one's strengths, values and aspirations amongst colleagues, peers, bosses for creating positive and beneficial influence.

- It helps in building mutual trust, supportive partnerships and cooperation in groups and organization.

Three Phases of branding process

Being confident and at ease with one self

Being confident and at ease with one self is the starting point of the self branding process. You might have come across people who are highly knowledgeable and competent in their field but they do not carry the sense of confidence and fail to make a great impression about themselves.

Apart from knowledge and skills our beliefs play an important role in making us confident about our positive values, strength, etc. In chapter 2 we have discussed in length about creating positive belief about oneself. For the process of branding to work for you there also have to be a positive belief about branding and projecting one self. I have come across people who believe that projecting oneself is some sort of manipulation. Naturally when you think this way you will never be at ease with yourself, while displaying your knowledge or skill in any type of test or interview. So first we need to examine our values and beliefs with regard to branding process.

Examining Values and Beliefs

A value is defined as something you consider important. For example, health, wealth, happiness, knowledge, growth, contribution, success, etc are all examples of values people have.

Now just take two minutes to think of some of your values and beliefs which support or hinder the branding process. Critically examine how you came to believe this over a period of time. In what ways your beliefs and values have helped you to promote your career aspiration and results. If you will examine closely, you will realize that in a way you have been presenting and branding yourself at all stages of your career. As a child you presented your talent and strengths to parents and that is why they created right kind of opportunities and environment for your career. Similarly you got involved in a prestigious school project because you could present your talents to your teachers. In fact the entire process of exams and the marks you get is the process of displaying your knowledge to the examiner, which helps you in being branded as a meritorious student and so on.

So you see there is nothing new in it, however we need to believe in the importance of this branding process in today's times of competition and more importantly being at ease while presenting ourselves and our unique strengths several times to prospective employers, examiners, customers, experts, superiors etc. We have to be mentally prepared for this process and take it with a sort of good nature and a sense of humour, rather than get either too tense or overly casual about the whole process. Incidentally, this also helps you in understanding your strengths and weakness and enables you to learn from the feedback provided by others. If in this process you realize you need to improve your credentials through a degree, certificate or a membership of a professional body then you will have to do that, so that you are in a strong position to present yourself with confidence and ease.

Getting used to the process and learning from it

Suppose you have to take an important exam after a few months. What ever be the subject matter of the exam, it will do you good if you experience a similar process several times before the real exam. This could be like a mock test which you should take every week to test how you are doing. Arrange to get the feedback so that you learn your mistakes, know how much time to spent on each question, how to identify easy question first rather than wasting time on tough ones etc . The timing of your mock test should preferably coincide with that of real one. For e.g. if the real test is going to be between 9-10 AM, then make sure your practice test are also at the same time every week. This way you would get attuned to the test process.

Similarly it helps, if you familiarize yourself with the interview process before the actual interview. I remember one interview in which a candidate had prepared a 30 minutes presentation, while the time allowed was only 10 minutes.

Obviously he was surprised and became nervous and so couldn't do well to the extent he could have. An often question at the start of interview is - Tell me about your self or some variation of this. This is something one should be ready to answer and the best way is to do it several times in front of mirror, friends and even presenting yourself to strangers, because most likely you are not going to find any acquaintances when you go for the interview. Here are some common and some uncommon ways for getting used to process of presenting yourself to the others.

Some common ways

- Speak about yourself in front of mirror
- List out your strengths and weakness & discuss with a colleague
- Practice a mock interview with a friend or colleague

Some uncommon ways

- Help a friend or acquaintance in selling services such as insurance/credit cards or help an NGO in donation drive.
- Make a presentation in a conference about your field of interest.
- Join a professional group and exchange views with members
- Make an actual bid for a part time project in a specific career field of your interest
- Work out an arrangement with an experienced professional offering him your help in a particular field
- Approach an organization for a summer project for a month or so.
- Make a presentation to friends/colleagues explaining recent trends and practices in career field of your interest
- Post your views on a career website and invite suggestions of fellow professionals

The basic idea of the approach is to first feel comfortable in talking to people about yourself and being at ease while talking to them. Over a period of time it is important to enjoy this process of talking to several people about yourself so that you learn the art of being natural and holding other's interest, whatever is the topic of discussion. Learning that comes from it is a bonus! Do not trust your memory and always make written notes about what you have learnt. This is all the more important if you are taking up the challenge of presenting yourself to others for the first time and are not used to the process.

Developing a creative focus

The starting point of all creative endeavors including that for career growth is the creative focus. Creative focus means harnessing the strength of all your mental faculties to circumvent any obstacle that comes in your way. Your generic Project helps you in getting that desired focus. Keeping the broad aspects of your GP, you may have to face certain specific situation-like a change in your job, when you find that you are stagnating in your present job. So one has to focus on a specific aspect of what could be a step towards your long term goal.

However there is a dissonant note in this. Have you ever observed that when you become vary narrowly focused on a goal and then find an insurmountable obstacle in front of you, you become very frustrated? Let me illustrate this with an example. Suppose you are a very religious person and have decided to go for a pilgrimage to the Shrine of Vaishnav Devi in Jammu & Kashmir. You are very focused and excited about this goal and this is really very important to you at this point of time. You reached upto Katra –the nearest motor able town. As you are just planning for the climb, you get the news that there has been a terrorist attack in the shrine and many pilgrims have been hurt. The way to the shrine is closed indefinitely and no one is allowed to visit the shrine.

Now, if you have a very narrow perspective of your goal, you will be overwhelmingly frustrated. However if you have a broader perspective of the goal, you will think that this is an opportunity to serve those pilgrims who have been hurt in the terrorist attack. So, you would help the victims, provide them all the relief, build a bonding with them and consider that this is the best way to pay your respect to the deity. Let us now see the characteristics of a people with a creative focus in their life.

Character sticks of a person with creative focus

1. Has clear focus and a broad view of the situation.
2. Values wisdom over cleverness.
3. Cultivates patience and strategic thinking when going gets tough.
4. Confident & decisive but humble.
5. Robust in thought but practical in approach.
6. Doesn't waste time in over intellectualization, or procrastination or dithering in decision.
7. Able to discern progress after examining the situation.
8. Practices and observes his thinking to develop his mental faculties.

In the above example the person who considers the work of helping the victims of the attack as equivalent or a better way of paying respect to the deity has a clear focus yet he does not defines his objective in a narrow way. He takes a broad view of the situation and therefore when he comes back home, he feels the satisfaction in recounting to his family members as to how he helped the other pilgrims. So, you see that getting the creative focus involves both clarity about your goals and a wider perspective about what those goals would mean under various trying circumstances.

Viewing your career interest in a flexible manner

Since your GP represents the general field of long term interest in accordance to the type of opportunities that you foresee for yourself in the future, therefore it gives you the desired flexibility to opt for jobs/career/tasks and projects which are likely to meet your career aspirations in terms of both career growth and job satisfaction. Contrary to this when you look at yourself in terms of particular field or job, you loose the option of moving into a new or emerging field because you tend to consider yourself as a person with limited choices based on your job or past experience. When

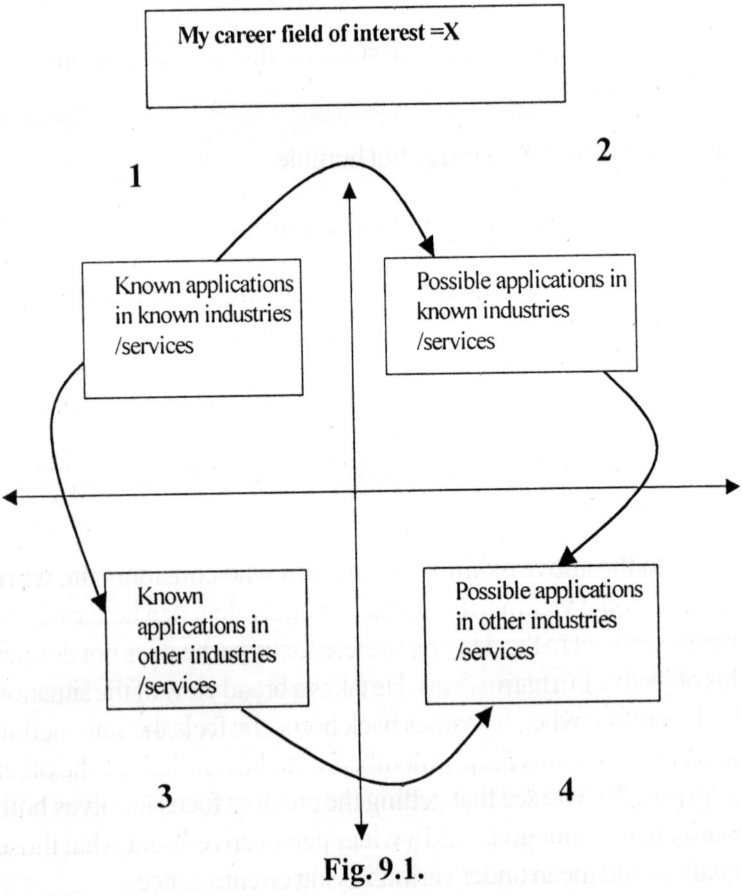

Fig. 9.1.

you look at your career interest from the perspective of your GP, it becomes easy for you to look it in a flexible manner so that you are open to all possible opportunities that are emerging in and around your area of interest. The diagram below shows how your area of interest may have many more applications beyond what you are familiar presently.

Let me illustrate importance of creative decision by an example. A friend of mine was desperate to change his career to a different industry about which his experience was negligible. He was a civil engineer with about 5 years experience of construction of residential complexes.

He was keen to join an organization that was into design and Construction of airports. It had many a lucrative project for Airport expansion, city side developments, design of intelligent buildings, airport terminals etc. The evening before he was going for the interview he considered his strengths and weaknesses and discussed these with his colleagues. His colleagues suggested many things. But basically their advice was all the same in one way or the other. To emphasize that he is a team player, has exposure to projects which could be considered similar to airports design and construction, and that he is great learner.

In the evening he thought over all these choices and realized that there is nothing greatly appealing about these, because the employer was looking for people with experience in airport. So he decided a novel approach based on his unique strength. While emphasizing all his strengths, he candidly admitted to the interviewer that he has hardly any knowledge or experience about airports. The interviewer was surprised and asked him –Why he applied for this job and he simply said, Sir – I am not here to contribute regarding that aspect about which your organization is already strong, I am here to contribute that which is my unique strength and that is – project management skills through which I can deliver results which are crucial for your organization. Then he reeled out his achievements relating to timely completion of projects and savings achieved in various projects. He demonstrated that similar improvements are also possible in Airport projects. The interviewer was quite impressed with his depth of knowledge and experience and he got the job.

Divergent thinking triggers for opening right doors

Many people have very set notions about how to go about making a break in their career field of interest or getting their dream job. The dominant mental pattern of many people seeking a career break is quite familiar- making a standard CV, making several copies of it and sending to several prospective employers. They forget that really effective decision come as a result of first generating several options through divergent thinking. Having created these options, we then need to use convergent thinking to focus on those that are most useful to the specific situation at hand, as shown in the diagram below.

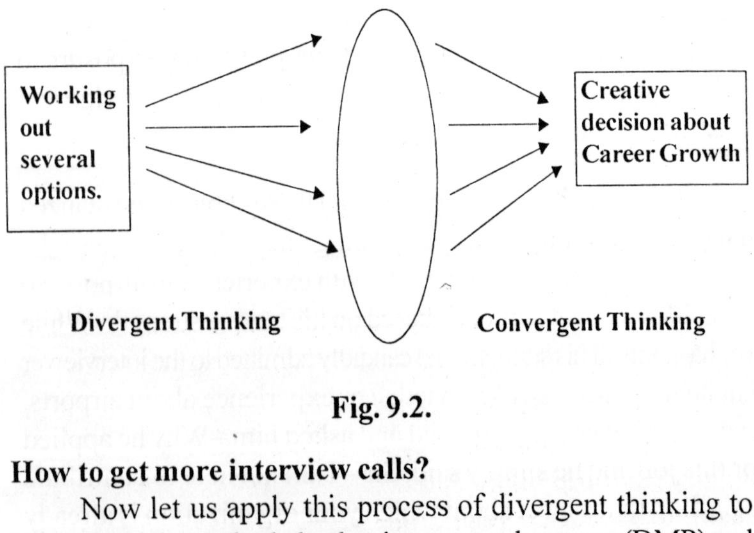

Fig. 9.2.

How to get more interview calls?

Now let us apply this process of divergent thinking to consciously list out both the dominant mental patterns (DMP) and

Out of dominant mental patterns (ODMP) to see what could be the different ways of getting more interview calls for a job.

This is illustrated in the Fig 9.3.

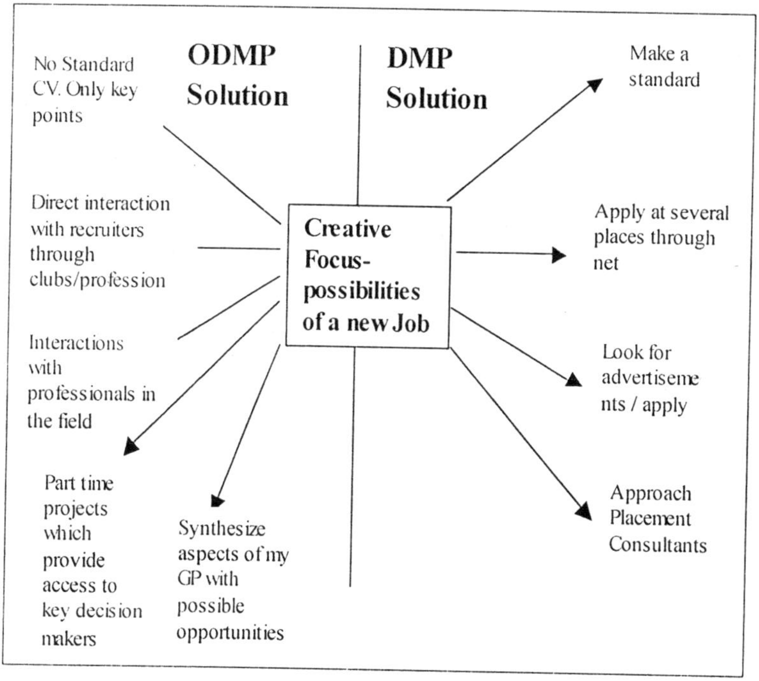

Fig 9.3

If you see the Fig 9.3, you will find that the right hand side of the diagram i.e out of DMP approach will be of great help in getting a lot of informal first hand information about what kind of job opportunities are suitable for you. This can also help you in keeping track of any new developments or opportunities in career field and areas of interest. This informal interaction with people can also help identify common grounds between yourself and the company you are going to approach. You can thus try to find out about the company-its people, values, culture etc. So, when you finally make your CV you can obviously emphasize this common ground between you and the target job.

Another important aspect which "Out of DMP approach" emphasizes -is to assess how far you are networked. Many good opportunities are never advertised but filled in through contacts and referrals. So it is important to look for opportunities to interact with fellow professionals, who can give you useful leads and information. You have to explore various ways in which you come in contact with right people or get to know them.

There are various ways to do this such as - professional membership, clubs, article in a professional magazine, professional visits, paper presentation in seminars etc to name a few. Incidentally these are also helpful in branding yourself. Such forums and opportunities help you in presenting yourself to others in a short period. Apart from participating in such forums, always think of such forums/ platforms as an opportunity to collect relevant information about areas of your interest. Whenever you are in such situation do not forget to collect the visiting cards of any person you meet and always make it a practice to give your visiting cards, so that you can easily contact each other whenever there is a need.

Initiating Contact for a Job or position

Many people rush to prospective employers with their CV, without even knowing whom to contact for what purpose. It is always a better practice to open yourself gradually in front of the prospective emplyer. First initiate interaction just to understand the right person to contact.Even when you know this, you must never rush your CV without understanding the interest of the other party. First understand the requirements and asses your suitability. Even if you have a ready made CV, which you have made after considerable thinking you must always customize it once again to emphasize the aspects that are more important to the present context. Here are a few points which should be kept in mind while making your CV.

How should your CV look like?

- Ideally relevant aspects about your credentials which have bearing on your candidature for a position must be covered in first page itself. Details can follow later or even in an annexure.

- A covering letter must always accompany the CV. Remember covering letter is important for developing rapport with people.

- Often covering letter is more important than the CV and many people do not go through the CV but make up their mind by going through the covering letter.

- Covering letter should be comprehensive one written in a professional style highlighting the salient aspects of your CV.

- Personal details at the end of CV should include all possible ways of contacting you through phone/email/ postal address etc. Include 2 references if possible.

Modeling the problem

Before we illustrate this with an example relevant to career aspects, let us briefly understand what problem modelling is. Problem modelling is the process of understanding all the aspects and factors contributing to the key problem and then trying to understand the interrelationship between each factor by connecting each aspect of the problem through cause and effect diagram. Through this process we are able to see the entire pattern of cause and effect relationship between the various factors and sub factors, understand the most important causes and develop the strategies for systematically removing these causes. Modelling of the problem is usually done after completing the process of collecting all the options using the DMP as well as the out of DMP mode of thinking.

Let us go back to the same example we have taken earlier i.e How to get more interview calls from prospective employer(s)? This time let us put the key problem as the centre of focus. In this case let us say the key problem is not getting enough opportunities for personal interviews with prospective employers.

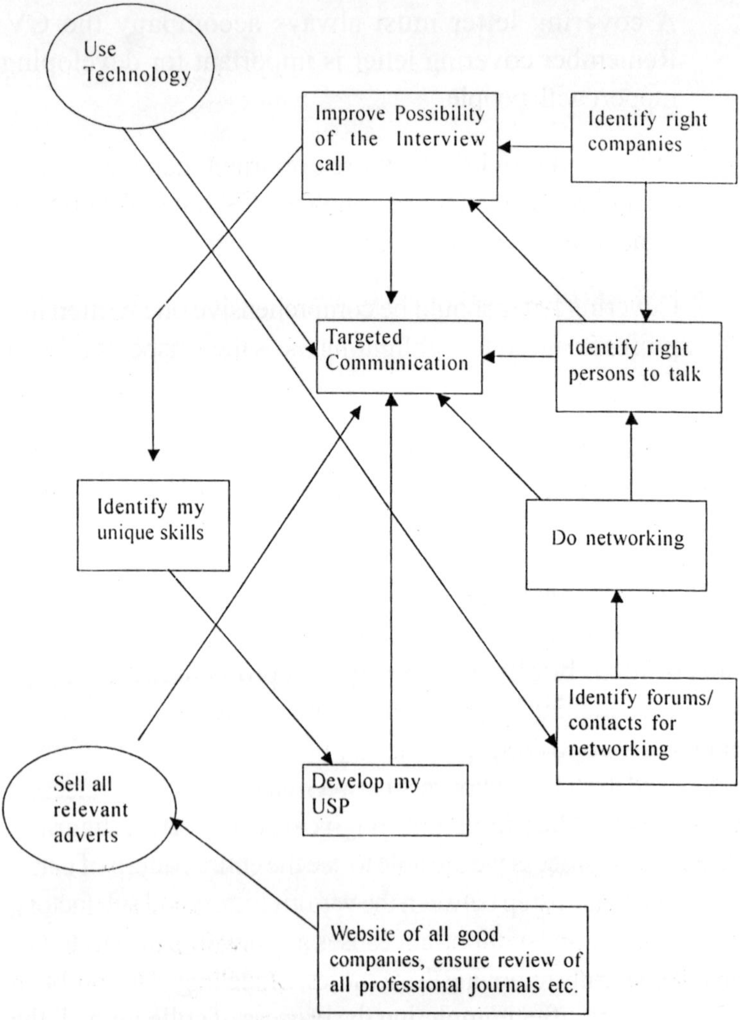

Fig. 9.4. Modelling the Problem.

Applying the approach to the problem of getting right interview calls?

Now when we look at Fig 9.4 , it becomes abundantly clear that the central issue which influences the solution to the problem to the greatest extent is "targeted communication", because it is one factor that has the most arrows pointed towards it. Having understood the central issue, we can develop a strategy to tackle this issue. We can now choose several attack points to deal with this problem. In the diagram above the arrows pointing to the central issues of "targeted communication" are the attack points that you need to deploy. In general you will see that there are two types of attack points in this case. One type can be said to be your internal focus and the others can be said to be the external focus. Based on this analysis following broad approaches may be used to improve your ability of "targeted communication" in an effective manner.

- Discuss with friends, colleagues and superiors to find out my unique strengths. If time permits take some self assessment tests

- Identify right persons for getting more information about the requirements in selected companies of my interest

- Develop my USP supported by whatever testimonials I have or can acquire over a period of time. USP means unique selling proposition, a term which marketing professional use to describe the unique selling points of their products or service.

- Build a portfolio to support my unique strength and work out creative ways to communicate through my CV/ covering letters.

- Prepare a questionnaire of all the likely questions that could be asked to me and my responses to these

- Identify all the companies that I will like to apply and make a habit of looking into their website once a week to identify new opportunities.

- Make a virtual group of non competing members and share information on regular basis.

- Subscribe a news paper/magazine that is likely to give me all details of advertisement in my field.

The above approach is just an illustration for a sample problem; your actual problem may be different from the one described above. However similar approach, starting with generation of several options followed by problem modelling will help you put systematic effort with a strategic focus to deal with the problem. When you work out your options always make it a point to consciously include both the Dominant as well as Non Dominant thinking pattern to arrive at solutions to your problem, so that you come up with more creative responses to the challenges in front of you.

Implementing Creative Decisions

As discussed previously divergent thinking will help you in determining all the options that are possible in your given situation. However once you have factored all the options related to your present problem, you will have to finally zero on to the specific decisions that you will like to take considering your specific situation in mind. This will require the process of convergent thinking i.e you need to converge to specific options out of the one's you consider plausible.

In the process of deciding, we often have to reject many such ideas which we do not find of much use. However, we must always be aware that every idea has some "Value" in it and even if 90% of an idea is valueless and impractical, our rejection of the idea also destroys the "value" in it. We throw the baby along with bath water. We need to learn the art of extracting the "value" from all the ideas that are available to us. So, when ever you get into the implementation mode, selecting a course of action from several options bewares of the tendency to reject any idea lock, stock and barrel. It may be worthwhile to examine, whether there is "some value" in the rejected ideas that may be possible to be synthesized in the final solution to your problem.

Effective negotiations for career growth

The negotiation process involves two or more parties with common as well as conflicting interst, who enter a process of interaction with the goal of reaching an agreement. The significance of negotiation skill is evident from the following quote by an eminent thinker.

"Everything we want seem to be in control of others"

-Roger Dawson

Negotiating process is important in any situation where the outcome for you is partially dependent on the other people. In that perspective most situations at work or career and even home involves some sort of negotiations with other people. Our normal approach to negotiations in any situation is to consider that the process starts at the time when there is actual discussion or contact between the two parties. However in reality negotiation process has hardly a well defined start or end time. The foundation of effective negotiations is almost always laid out at the preparatory phase. It is in the preparatory phase that you try to build "possible scenarios" of a future state that is beneficial to you as well as to the other party.

We are negotiating all the time-in our homes with spouse and children, in office with boss, colleagues and subordinates etc. In fact it is very much possible to see your entire career as a series of negotiations to meet your needs for getting the desired exposure, training courses and projects so that you are able to gain the required advantage for career growth and job satisfaction.

There are many situations in the day to day life which provide you the opportunity to hone your skills in the art of negotiations. Since the art of negotiations, is always learnt over a period of time it is important that we feel at ease with it and practice it constantly so that we are adept at its use when the big time arrives.

Understanding the mental model of the other party

Developing a good rapport and understanding is a pre-condition for negotiating win-win solutions with the other party be it- the interviewer, boss or anyone with whom you need to negotiate for advancing your career. Rapport is an understanding and trust between two people, which often happen at the unconscious level. It is much easy to convince or influence other people when you already have an excellent rapport with them.

Have you ever observed a group of people in a huddle during informal discussion during lunch hours or tea time in the office? If you observe such a huddle closely you will invariably see that the group members unconsciously start using similar gestures, phrases, jokes, tone etc as they become more familiar with each other. In fact this sense of mirroring of each other's behaviour and sharing a common style is indicative of rapport between members of the group. When people are in rapport with each other they tend to imitate each other's postures, tone, gestures and phrases more often. On the contrary when people are "out of sync" with each other, it is also reflected in mismatch between their behaviour pattern and style. This mismatch between two groups of people is often summarized in such generalized terms such as generation gap, different typecast etc.

Let me illustrate the importance of rapport in a corporate situation by recounting an interesting anecdote that I witnessed in a large public sector organization, where I was doing a consulting assignment Prakash, a newly joined middle level executive working in corporate HR in this organization was reporting to DGM (HR). He was however often called by the GM directly, for monitoring of important assignments particularly in the absence of his immediate boss. Though Prakash was doing his best, yet he observed that often the GM seemed to be unhappy or not satisfied by the reported progress on important assignments that he was handling. Prakash was always ill at ease, whenever the GM asked him something or the other on phone or in person. He was unable to understand what was causing this?

One day Prakash was having a cup of tea with his collegue and good friend Ravindra in the office. They were just having some informal talks and discussion, when Ravindra got a call in his intercom. Apparently the GM was on the other side, enquiring about progress on some key aspect. Ravindra responded in the following manner to the boss's querry.

"Sir, we have sent a total of 157 letters covering 100% of the targeted Sr.executives; out of which we have got the positive response from 97. 12 have expressed their inability to attend the conference and they will be sending the fax through their controlling officer. We are following up with the rest and I will keep you updated on that"

That Ravindra could satisfy the boss with his reporting was evident from the delightful grin in his face. Prakash was both envious and surprised to see Ravindra's confidence in reporting things to boss. He couldn't help but let out his curiosity in front of him. The following conversation took place between them.

Prakash: how do you recall all those numbers which you just rattled out to the boss? I noticed you didn't even look at the files, Do you really remember all these things?

Ravindra: Bursting into a hearty laugh- Dear, it all comes through experience. See, you are new in this department and do not understand the boss's nature. Boss likes everything in numbers. Once you give him some numbers he will be happy. I may not remember everything but I don't bluff either, the numbers I am giving may be approximate, however I am sure it will satisfy the boss.

Later prakash conferred to me that this chance learning was an eye opener for him. He realized that his style of reporting was a complete mismatch to the boss's mental model and therefore there was a lack of rapport between the two. In the words of prakash-

"I was using a lot of English in my reporting whereas the boss was interested in numbers. My descriptive and sophisticated style was completely at variance with his down to earth and fast paced style of talking and that is what was causing this sense of uneasiness whenever I interacted with him. In fact I was beginning to think that the boss was prejudiced against me and did not like me, when the only reason was that his mental model was different than mine. It is now evident that the Boss has a mental model, which equates too much description and preliminaries as sign of tardy progress. He is more satisfied when the progress is reported in brief, to the point and with numbers".

Prakash later modified his style to suit the boss's requirement and went in to establish an excellent rapport which helped him greatly in shaping his career. Eventually he left the organization and rose to the position of Head of HR in a reputed private sector organization. One thing which contributed to such a stupendous rise was his ability to negotiate for his involvement in high visibility and growth assignments, thus getting good exposure in key areas where there is a high demand for Senior HR professionals.

This anecdote illustrates the importance of understanding the other person mental model for creating a positive rapport and influencing others. More, often we keep trying to influence others by what is our favourite approach & style, without realizing that every individual is different and sees the world according to his mental model. When we observe other people keenly, we would be able to know whether we are on the same wave length and whether the other person is open to be influenced by us.

A Kellogg business school research states that one of the cues for social bonding is the unconscious awareness of being in "sync" with the other person. This unconscious awareness of a positive bonding can be triggered by consciously matching the other person's behavioural patterns during interactions. Matching and mirroring of behaviour are the main component for creating good rapport which is the right starting point for influencing others. The main component of behaviour that we can match and mirror include- Body postures and actions, Tone of voice, breathing pattern and key words and phrases.

Pacing and Leading

Pacing and Leading refers to the behavioural processes that happen during influencing. Pacing happens when you "match" the other person, which means that you consciously follow similar behaviour and style as that of the other person. However, while this is just the outward part, the basic idea of pacing is to enter the other person's model of the world and follow his thinking and feeling, so as to get a complete understanding of his mental model and its significance for evolving a win-win solution for both. If you pace someone and think cleverly you will not only understand his priorities, concerns, issues etc but you would also be able to see why and to what extent these things are important to him.

The interesting part is that once sufficient pacing has been done and there is better understanding of the person's concerns and issues, then the pacer can do a role reversal and begin to lead the other person. In this context, it can therefore be said that if you really want to lead somebody first follow him.

Many interesting applications of pacing and leading can be found in our daily life including in our families. Have you observed the difficulty parents today face in influencing their children? Often, parents try to influence and lead their children with their sermons and advice without first following and understanding their world. That is why they find it so hard to influence their children the way they want to groom and develop them. Many good teachers, coaches and mentors are naturally adept at this art of pacing and leading, although they may not be consciously aware of these terms. They are able to develop an excellent rapport with their pupil, by walking alongside them appreciating and understanding their mental model. This ability to walk alongside like a friend provides them the cue for a possibility of leading them appropriately when the pupil is ready to be influenced.

Whether a person being paced could now be influenced and lead, can be inferred by an interesting test that you can do it yourself. After mirroring and matching the person for a while, try to change your posture to a different way; if the other person starts following you, it is a clear indication that he is now mentally prepared for being influenced by you. Similarly use of phrases or metaphors (which are typical of you) by the other person is also an indicator that the other person is open for being influenced by you.

Some common fallacy about the negotiating process

- Negotiation is something that has to be reserved for a special situation like applying for a job interview or negotiating for a price or salary etc.

- Negotiation process has a clearly defined start time and an end time.

- Negotiation skills are inherent and can not be learnt.
- We are at great disadvantage when negotiating with authority figures, prospective employers or members of interview boards etc.
- In any negotiation situation it is best to spell out all our needs at one go and just wait for other side to respond.
- In any negotiating situation peoples real needs are the same as what they are openly stating.

Your ability to negotiate depends on the knowledge of the situation

In any negotiating process concerning your career, it is most important to know your immediate and long term needs. However it is equally important to have all possible relevant information about the situation. In fact in a job situation it becomes so easy for you to get the relevant information when you have a friend working in the same company. Just imagine the advantage you get when you know what type of people is going to be in the interview board. What type of experience and skills the company is looking for etc?

That is why it is always preferable to apply for career growth through known sources as far as possible. Even when you do not have a known contact in the company, you can always try to gather the information by talking to present or past employees/ vendors/ customers/ any trainer or consultant who have been providing their service to the organization etc. Often one contact cam lead to other and you will surely be able to get some meaningful information if you are persistent and patient about the whole thing.

In all negotiations there are mainly two types of things that are being bargained for, the first one being those needs and issue that are stated openly and the second are those which are the real needs of the people which are seldom stated openly. Do not forget that behind the façade of their institutional authority and arrogance, there are ordinary human beings who are desperately trying to meet their needs. For. e.g the HR department which has advertised for a position has target date to complete the recruitment and provide the new recruit to the department which has raised this demand.

There could be projects which may be getting neglected because key people have left and the organization is desperate to get the right people. There may be a mandate by their board to complete a restructuring process, create new positions and fill the positions by a certain date etc.The more you know these things the more you are in a position to negotiate effectively towards getting the desired results.

Apart from their real needs there are also many latent fears in the mind of a future employer which are not easily revealed. There is obvious concern in the minds of the future employers when there is a weak match between the job requirements and the credential of a candidate. But even when there is a strong match between credentials of a candidate and the job position, there still can be fears such as

- Whether the candidate will really join the organization when given an offer
- Whether the candidate will really stick to this organization for some time or is it just a short term arrangement for him.
- Is the candidate overqualified for the job and will feel frustrated later
- Whether the candidate will fit into our culture and able to contribute effectively within the context of our typical situation

Knowing these concerns or even making a reasonable guess will enable you to project yourself and negotiate in a manner so as to allay these fears to the extent possible. For e.g have you noticed a simple question at the end of Application blank of most companies that says –how much time you will take to join if selected? I have seen answers ranging from a week to about 3 months. When your answer is something like a week or as soon as I get the offer, you appear to be desperate about getting the job. Similarly when you answer this – 3 months, it appears that you hardly consider this as a priority. As a rule it is always better to give a time frame of 3 weeks, a month or maximum one and half month. You can always ask for more time if the situation so demands. Based on the above analysis, I will like to propose following three postulates of Negotiations.

1. If you can establish a reasonable guess about the other party's needs and apprehensions you can predict with remarkable certainty, what will be eventual outcome of a negotiation process?

2. In any negotiation based process the job/ position/contract or project goes to the person whose credentials are closest match to the requirements and not necessarily to candidate with the best credentials for it.

3. One of the best ways to prove that your credentials are closest match is to have an open mind and display a flexible approach to the issues and concern of the other party.

Your ability to negotiate depends on your perceived power

In any negotiating situation concerning your career, always understand that your ability to influence the other party depends on your perceived power. Your perceived power always improves when you enter the negotiating process with more than one option. If you enter any negotiation process without any other options the other party will often treat you lightly. By creating several options (however far fetched they may be) and hinting about these discretely and tactfully you can create a competition between different parties.

Much of your perceived power depends on how you establish your credentials at the early part of the interactions. You must remember that your credentials comprise of not only those aspects which you have achieved in the past but also in proving that similar or better achievements are likely to follow in the next job, project or situation. Your perceived power therefore depends on whether you appear to be the part of the solution (to their problems, concerns requirements etc) or you appear to be part of their future problems.

Always remember that your perceived power not only depends on your competencies and credentials but also includes any other resources which you can access such as professional network, vendors, consultants, experts etc. It is important to give hints about your resourcefulness during the course of interaction, because being resourceful is the easiest way to demonstrate your ability to solve problems and issue concerning the other party. Similarly, when you are unable to answer a question or concern about an issue, indicate that you have adequate resources and expert advice available to deal with it appropriately.

Your ability to negotiate depends on correct timings

For any negotiating situation concerning your career whether asking for a raise or a favourite assignment or even trying for a new job, timming is every thing. A friend of mine told me this important story about how he negotiated for signing of an order of raise by his boss. The boss was very happy, he was about to leave for Tokyo in a weeks time for a long assignment. My friend who worked with him took over the charge of his tickets and all sundry arrangements prior to the trip. The previous evening to his departure he came up with the typed order and requested him to sign. The boss couldn't refuse and he got the raise.

The best outcome can be achieved with patience and perseverance and having your options open all the time.

A checklist for Win-Win Negotiations

Developing the skill for win-win negotiation require patience and persistence. Keep the following checklist in mind whenever you need to enter into a negotiation process with others.

- Be prepared to go into discussions with a general goal and be flexible about your specific objective within the goal
- Do your home work well about your needs and priorities but avoid having any preconceived bottom line
- Ask frequent questions about the other party's goals and priorities
- Look for better and effective ways rather than your way for reaching an agreement.
- Explore other party's objectives and search for common ground.
- Be open about what you hope to achieve and be persistent and patient in your approach
- Your primary aim must be look for an effective solution and not necessarily the amicable solution
- Agree to disagree if you find something unacceptable, rather than rushing for an agreement
- Explore the reasons for difference of opinion, if any.

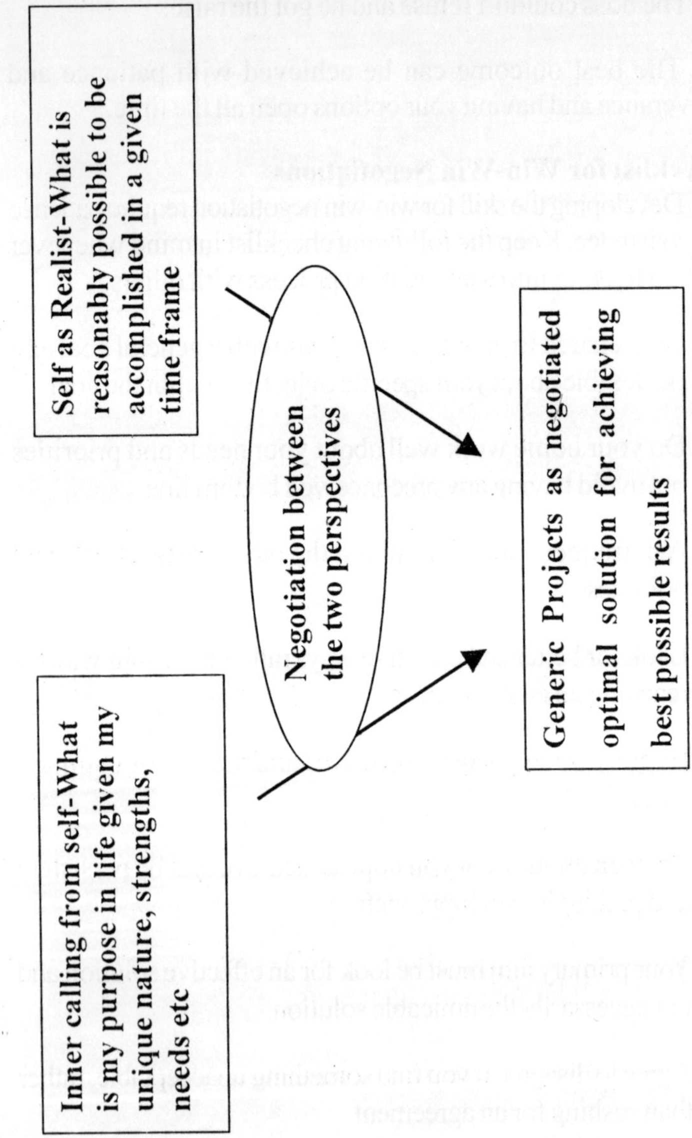

Fig. 9.5. GP as Negotiated Optimal Solutions.

- Confront the problem and not the person

Win-Win approach to mutually satisfying negotiations

If you have done the exercise in chapter III, you would realize that your Generic projects (GP) represent is the negotiated settlement between what you truly consider your inner calling and what you consider as practical for a meaningful career and livelihood.

Just like negotiations with other parties involve some adjustment on your part, similarly negotiation with self also involves some adjustments and adaptability on your part so that your plans are realistic and economically viable to support you and your family.

Negotiating for your dream job

Follow the steps discussed below to gather relevant information and working out a winning strategy.

- Identify certain companies / jobs/ projects or locations etc in which you dream of making a career for your self. Let this list be as long as you think feasible. You may like to refer to exercise designing your GP in chapter III. Collect information about each of these regarding their recruitment system for areas /functions of interest to you.

- Identify formal sources of information such as web sites, professional magazines, recruitment consultants, HR departments, PR departments etc and keep a ready reckonner of all the important contact numbers for systemic enquiry and recording.

- Identify informal sources like friends, contacts, professional memberships, clubs, vendors, customers, or any one who could provide contact details of their friends or acquaintances working in that field or company. You can also look for information in the net through search engines/informal blog etc. An excellent source of information is colleges or institution from where the company has been recruiting.

- Visit these "places of interest" during lunch time or after formal office hours once a while and cultivate informal contacts with people who are working there. Another creative way of knowing more about the company of your choice is by creating a context which is other than their recruitment process. For fresher passing out from educational institute, discussing possibility of summer projects and internship provides an excellent context to develop informal contacts and collect the relevant information about the company.

- Even if you are not a fresh pass out you can still contact the company on behalf of a friend or younger brother etc and this will enable you to know more about the company in a completely non guarded manner. Many organizations participate in community development activities as part of their CSR (corporate social responsibility) endeavour. Since many such activities are participatory in nature, one can also explore possibilities of involving or at least enquiring about such activities.

- Similarly always make it a point to visit trade fair or exhibition where your company of choice may be represented to know more about the company, its product and services etc.

Though you may have to spend some time in the process but it will obviously helpful in providing leads and contacts for influencing your prospects with the company. Once you have some reasonable information about the company, try to correlate the formal information with informal information and try to build a picture of the company and career prospects for you.

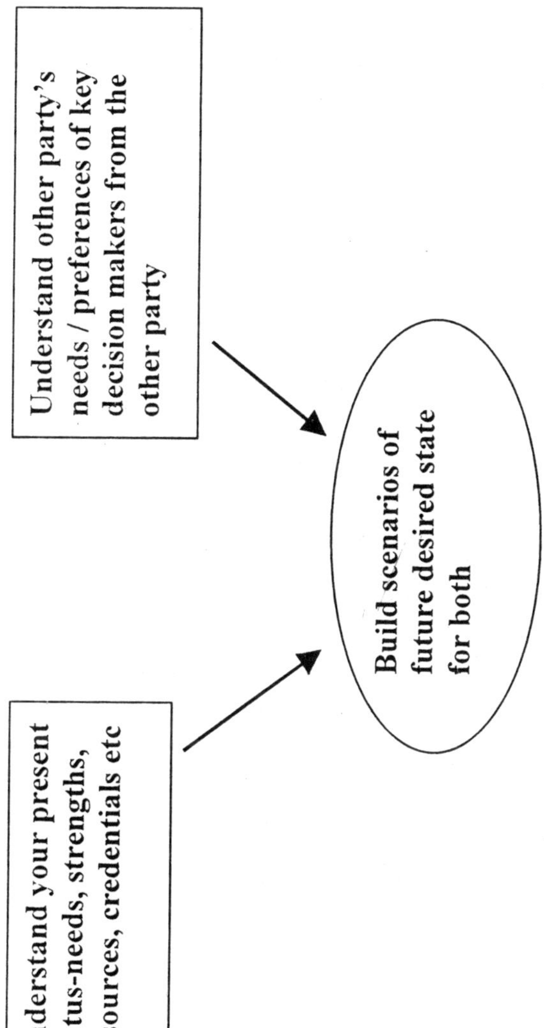

Fig. 9.6. Building Win-Win Scenarios.

The above approach underlines the importance of considering negotiation as a process which starts much earlier than the actual discussions takes place. Take for example an application for job position in a company. Many candidates do not do proper homework before applying for a job position. Proper homework means trying to get as much information about the needs and requirements of the company that you wish to join. It also means to try to understand the preferences of the key decision maker through informal sources to the extent possible. This process is shown in fig 9.6.

The "possible scenarios" that your draw for the future must be such that it is beneficial to you while also takes care of the needs and requirements of the other party. Some time it may be possible that the other party is represented by many diverse interests and it may be difficult to know what is really of interest to them. Even in that case it is utmost important to know how the preferences of the "key decision makers" from the other side can effect the outcomes of the decisions of the negotiation process.

Fig 9.7

The exercise given below will help you plan this approach in case of your applying or approaching a company for a job interview.

Exercise: Planning for a win-win negotiation with an Organization

Understanding the needs and requirements of the organization

What are the needs and requirements of the specific organization or similar organization types (based on type of industry/sector etc?). Prepare a check list of formal and Informal sources as given below. Place a (√) besides the ones that are applicable in your specific case.

Sources	*Organization Specific*	*Industry or Sector related*
Formal	• Web sites • Professional magazines • Recruitment consultants • HR departments • PR departments • Placement consultant	• Industry Association • Professional Bodies • Professional magazines • Research Institutes • Placement Consultant
Informal	• Friends • Contacts • Memberships • Clubs • Colleges or Institutes from where the company has been recruiting	• Competitors • Contacts • Memberships • Clubs • Vendors, Customers • Blogs

Approaching the organization informally

Many people send their CV as quickly as possible when they spot a good job opportunity. It is often a good idea to approach the organization or the consultant (if they are hiring thorough one) informally before you send in the formal application. This can always be done for seeking some clarification about your candidature while also trying to assess your prospects, the nature of competition or any other important information which you have failed to obtain during your independent research. When approaching the organization informally, talk to lower level people first because often they are more open then senior level officers. Of course everybody in the company can be important source of information at that time. A very useful idea at this stage is to make a personal visit to the organization during lunch time and speak informally to the concerned persons asking for help in understanding the requirements for the job position. At the end of this stage you must have some idea of a few things relating to your prospects and possible time frame for the start and completion of the negotiation process.

- To what extent this is a priority for the organization
- Is there at least some initial interest for your candidature
- Will it be worthwhile to consider this as an important priority and focal area for your job search
- If the answer to above question is Yes, then what is likely to be the approximate time frame for being called for a meeting or personal interview
- What is likely to be the total time period for culmination of this selection process

Build possible scenarios

- Write a script on behalf of the other party based on your research of their needs and requirements. You may include preferences of key decision makers if possible.

- Write a script on behalf of yourself based on research of your needs and requirements.

Using the information collected build 2-3 possible scenarios that are likely to happen as a result of your interaction with the organization. Collect additional information if so required and write briefly your expectations based on research carried out by you.

At this stage it is also useful to work out all possible options that you would like to explore while interacting with the other party.

Plan for formal meeting

Customize your CV or letter in accordance with the above analysis for this particular organization. Emphasize that aspects of your credentials and experience which are in line with the organization's requirements and needs. Even your covering letter must be written in a manner to give a positive hope about a future desired state that is beneficial to both you and the organization to which you are applying for a job position. Prepare a list of all the possible questions that the interviewer may like to know from you and be prepared to answer these.

If possible arrive 10-15 minutes earlier for the meeting so that you can know the name and background of key people who are likely to be in the interview so that you can build a positive rapport during your interaction. One very important aspect of developing rapport is to try to use similar expressions or word that is used by the other person. Similarly it is important to mirror their postures and style of speaking for creating a better rapport. Remember the importance of the face to face interaction is to understand the preferences of key decision makers besides also conveying what you consider is important for you. Do not speak for too long and wait for the others to speak as well. Be prepared to modify your approach (if need be) on the basis of addition information during the meeting.

An excellent way to prepare your mind for seeking all possible options is to explore an ongoing professional relationship with key decision makers and marking out areas of mutual interest.

The Closing Rituals and future prospects

- Collect contact details of all you have interacted, particularly the email. A job interview is an excellent opportunity to make new professional friends who are sailing in the same boat as yours.
- Seek feedback from selected few about how you were perceived.
- Send Thanks note to all with whom you had an opportunity to interact.
- Keep contact alive with selected few about 6 months or more if required.
- Document your learning from the feedback.
- Keep it in writing because often we tend to forget to learn from experience if we do not document it properly.

One of the key outputs of your formal meetings should be generation of some more alternatives even when your candidature is found to be unsuitable for the job position.

10

Pro-active Planning for Execution Excellence

A balanced perspective is important for anybody who wishes to make a great and rewarding career. There is a story about a student who was considered extremely bright by his teachers due to his extraordinary ability in math and science. The bright student was expected to make a great career as engineer after passing out from school but he couldn't, because he failed in Hindi. All that was needed by this student was to spare a little time for his Hindi lessons so that he could manage to pass the exam but since the student was not guided properly he lost one valuable year from his career and also became disheartened and depressed.

If you wish to plan for a rewarding and successful career it is utmost important to develop a balanced perspective about other related aspects such as family, health, financial aspects etc. "Balanced" does not mean that all the aspects must be considered of equal importance, however what it does mean is that one must consider all the relevant aspects which have a bearing on our well being and overall effectiveness. Neglecting a particular aspect of life may start affecting other related aspects and that may include career growth also. For example a person who neglects his health would have trouble in putting in good effort in his job or a person in huge financial crisis would have difficulty in concentrating on his studies or job.

A balanced perspective is important because it helps you see the total reality, when viewing your career growth and prospects. When you are able to see the total reality with undivided and unfragmented way, your behavior also becomes more wholesome and the responses are geared to take into account key and important area that are crucial to maintain tranquility in the face of numerous pressures of our competitive times.

The exercise given below is designed to help you in mastering the skills of proactive planning for execution excellence. Follow this 5 steps exercise to develop a specific yet flexible plan for achieving your key goals.

Exercise: Proactive planning for execution excellence

1. A balanced approach to Long term planning

Define your key goals from balanced perspectives (for about 6 months to a year). Remember to make your goals "SMART" i.e. Specific, Measurable, Achievable, Realistic and Time bound.

Sl.No	*Perspective(s)*	*Key goals*	*Aprox end dates*
1.	Family		
2.	Career		
3.	Financial		
4.	Any others(S)		

Use the format given below to specify one key goal under each of the perspectives given below. So, mark about 3-4 key goals as A, B, C & D for ease of reference and also specify an approximate end dates for each.

Identify blockages

List all possible blockages that can come in the way of achieving your above goals. Now categorize all the blockages that you have listed into the four categories as given below. You may take the help of a friend or partner for this part. A brief description of each of the blockages is as given below for ease of reference.

(a) Cliff- A real blockage, which may be extremely tough to handle without support form experts/authorities/institutions or resourceful people etc.

(b) Hill- A tough blockage which may require support of your friends and well wishers.

(c) Hedge- A barrier which is due to your own attitudes, inhibition or past experience etc.

Type	*Brief description of Blockage(s) for each of key goals*			
	Goal A	*Goal B*	*Goal C*	*Goal D*
Cliff				
Hill				
Hedge				
Fog				

d) Fog – A barrier due to attitude or mindset of people around you.

Check your perceptions

- Discuss your above perceptions regarding the blockages with a good friend or colleague and redo the above list based on objective understanding of each blockage.

- However if after this also you find too many Cliffs (2 or more for a particular goal). Go back to the concerned goal, modify and redefine it to make it moderately difficult rather than extremely tough.

- Similarly if there are too little hills, you may again go back and redefine to include slightly more challenging goals.

2. My Get Going Action Plan (this week/ next week/this month)

Generate a 3 digit code for each of your proposed initiatives for handling the blockages. The 1st digit for the goals i.e. A, B, C & D. The 2nd digit for initiative Types (Sl. No as given in table below) and the 3rd category for your specific initiative, in your own words

Sl. No.	*Initiative Types*	*Your specific initiative in your own word*	*Code*
1.	Resource mobilization	This is an initiative which will help generate resources for dealing with both goals A & B simultaneously. The code on the right hand column reflects this.	AB11
2.	Networking & generating support		

(Contd.)

(Contd. Table)

Sl. NO	*Initiative Types*	*Your specific initiative in your own word*	*Code*
3.	Involving Authorities /experts		
4.	Collecting information		
5.	Being better organized		
6.	Building mutual trust		
7.	Studying and gaining knowledge		
8.	Learning new skills /techniques		
9.	Developing positive habits / self Belief		
10.	Identifying experts/ knowledge sources		
11.	Improving efficiency and energy level		
12.	Any other		

(a numeral). An initiative pertaining to two goals simultaneously can also be codified by including both the goals in the code. For e.g an initiative under resource mobilization pertaining to both the goals A & B simultaneously may be codified as AB11. This is shown as an example in the table below. Now complete this table to include as many initiatives that come to your mind.

3. Detailed Goal Wise Planning

Now select one important Goal at a time to do a detailed planning. You may also take up a composite goal codified as "AB", if you find that many initiatives are jointly applicable to both of them simultaneous.

Now rate each of the codified initiatives as key priorities from the three perspectives of :

1. Happiness- Will be a source of great personal satisfaction for me
2. Critical edge-Will provide a critical edge for achieving this goal
3. Learning Value- Has a great learning value for me
4. Timing- Is important because of timing consideration

For each of your goal, rate each of proposed initiative from the three perspectives given above.

Initiative Code	*Ratings on each perspective*				*Overall Priority*
	Happiness	*Critical edge*	*Learning Value*	*Is the time Right?*	

Trigger Plan – For getting best out of windows of opportunities

This plan must unfold when there is a "expected favourable development" at a future date.

Initiative Code	*Ratings on each perspective*				*Overall priority*
	Happiness	*Critical edge*	*Learning Value*	*What time is Right?*	

Contingency Plan – For preparing for a likely contingency

This plan must unfold when there is a "likely contingency" at a future date.

Initiative Code	*Ratings on each perspective*				*Overall priority*
	Happiness	*Critical edge*	*Learning Value*	*What time is Right?*	

When planning each of above initiative ask following probing questions to self.

- What time is best suited for each activity in particular day, morning, evening etc.
- What preparatory activity will make the initiative and attendant tasks smooth and efficient?

- What initiative is such that it will require patience and some effort every day for a period of time?
- What initiative is such that it will require prior knowledge of other's views, past decision, willingness and acceptance of others to be really effective?
- What initiative is such that its exact requirements are not known at the moment but depend on other parallel development. If so what part or preparatory activity can be taken up now?
- What initiative is so critical that a single mistake can cost a lot so each and every aspect has to be thoroughly examined before giving it a final shape?
- What initiative will relieve you of lot of pain and unnecessary work and free you for more important work /favourite activity
- What initiative will help me respond to windows of opportunities or likely contingency better?

4. Setting Clear Mile Stones

Having set your goals and understood the barriers to achieving them, set specific milestones that you wish to reach w.r.t each of your goals in order to be satisfied about your progress. While setting these milestones, remember the well-formed conditions of the clear goals (pl. refer to chapter 5). You must specify the milestones in clear and unambiguous term. Actually it is quite similar to the mile stone you actually see while you travel to a destination. You must specify a milestone to answer the question – what will I see, hear, and feel so that I am convinced that I am getting closer to my destination. Mark these milestones in specific terms in a calendar or quarterly planner in your dairy, so that you may review your progress later and take corrective actions when required.

5. Review progress

Review your progress on weekly or fortnightly basis to check your progress and add new initiatives to deal with any contingency that may arise. Repeat the cycle on quarterly basis to modify goals as per the changing circumstances and new opportunities that are emerging or that comes to your mind as you do the Trigger plan and contingency plan as specified above.

Preparing for transition times

Today's world is characterized by constant change and unpredictability. These changes are due to several factors such as political, economic, social, and technological as well as change in Government policies etc. Organizations, world over continue to respond to this challenge by restructuring to adapt to these changes. Such restructuring can also affect the job market and career prospects for individuals. Many people may loose their jobs due to restructuring and downsizing. For example the recent appreciation of rupee against dollar has squeezed the margins for many BPO and IT firms. This in turn has lead to cost cutting, downsizing and layoffs.

During the course of you career growth, sometime you may find that things are stable and going on in a smooth and predictable manner. There are also times when there is a lot of change around you. It is not only the changes in your work environment that can affect your career but even changes at the family front, and personal circumstances can also have an impact on your career.

These changes are brought out by external factors over which we may not have much control. Sometime a change may auger well for our career and at other times the change may completely overwhelm us and make us depressed and miserable. However if we learn the art of responding to these changes appropriately we may not only be able to survive but also thrive in the midst of these changes. Our ability to cope with the change would also enable us respond to new opportunity that change brings rather than feel anxious and worried. How we think, feel and respond to these changes has strong implication for our career in the long run. So, here is an exercise (a set of thought provoking questions) which will help you in introspecting and responding appropriately to changes around you.

Exercise: Facilitating transition and managing change

Consider the changes in your personal circumstances and work environment in the recent past or within the last 1-2 years and now answer the following questions.

1. Have I considered the impact of these changes in my career or work life? What is likely to be different?

2. Am I going to learn something important as a result of this change process? What is it?

3. Which aspects have aggravated the "feelings of loss" due to change process?

4. Has the loss due to change process been very painful and if so have I reconciled myself to the situation by observing my feelings and responses through support of close friends etc?

5. Is it affecting my sense of self confidence and belief about myself and if so what professional help and support, I may need to overcome the sense of loss.

6. Have I stopped and reflected on the continuities in my life and done something to strengthen them.

7. Am I actively engaged in accessing information, negotiating, arranging support and resources to prepare for the transition times?

8. Have I created a "Zone of stability" (in the form of a good habit, spiritual practice etc) in the midst of the chaos unleashed by the change process?

9. Have I set aside sometime to take stock of my present life now both in relation to the goals I had set before the change process started and now in terms of my present aspirations and needs, which might help me to set other important goals?

10. What new possibilities are emerging for me, given my abilities, resources and core strengths?

11. Have I reassessed my GP in the light of these changes and is my GP aligned to the new situation?

12. Am I asking thought provoking new questions to myself or Am I stuck in a stereotype thinking pattern?

13. Am I exploring new possibilities, discussing and debating on possible workable options?

14. Am I looking at coincidences, analogies etc for my new situation and trying to decipher meaning for purposeful action?

15. Do I write out 3 positive outcomes of the day before I retire for sleep?

16. Have I set in some key priorities for the immediate to restore my sense of self confidence and achievement in me?

17. Have I set in some specific short term target to get going and restore sense of movement?

18. Am I consciously taking time for regular exercise so as to maintain my health and energy level?

19. Am I cultivating some hobbies for rejuvenating myself to get out of the stereotyped pattern being forced on me by my present circumstances?

20. Am I maintaining harmonious relationships with people around me and getting their cooperation in every possible way?

Ponder over the Reponses you get to each of the above questions, discuss with a good friend, partner or mentor and find ways to convert all of these to a positive response. Out of all the above questions specially look at Questions 7-11, 15-18 and 20 and try and give your best possible response to these questions.

Mastering execution skills

The people who have a successful and rewarding career are those who plan proactively rather than reacting to various contingencies and developments as they arise. Proactive planning helps in building self commitment, strong motivation and energy for their goals. It also helps in visualizing and identifying opportunities, challenges and bottlenecks. This facilitates better response to "windows of opportunities" as also in dealing with contingencies that are likely to impede their progress while executing key objectives.

During the times of change particularly during difficult times when we are down and low, it is important for us to be aware of our thinking pattern, our feelings and responses and constantly challenge these by posing insightful questions and reflecting on them. Such reflections often help us in seeing things with fresh perspective and help us in developing a positive mental framework to respond better to the challenges posed by the changes.

One key test to indicate whether you are learning and evolving all the time is to check whether you experience a certain level of anxiety while carrying out your plans and activities. If you do not feel any anxiety you may not be taking appropriate level of challenge and you may be becoming dull and stereotyped. A certain level of anxiety is good and is indicator that you are learning and taking on reasonable challenge. However if the anxiety increases too much it may indicate that you are getting too ambitious and this is certain to cause bad stress which would eventually effect your health and peace of mind.

Setting targets, seeing them clearly and achieving them builds our confidence in our abilities and encourages us to set further challenging targets. This essentially is the process of career growth also. While the exercises in this chapter are designed to help you in mastering the skills of proactive planning for execution excellence, the ones that follow are designed to help you develop your support network.

Developing your support network

It is estimated that new knowledge that is created in the last one decade is equivalent to that created in the preceding 50 years. The pace of change in every sphere of human activity is so fast that it is extremely difficult to keep track of it.

There is so much happening in today's dynamic world that it is practically impossible to take account of all the developments that can have an impact on your career or work life. In the ever changing milieu of economic growth and new trends, it is utmost impossible for any one person to keep track of the possible opportunities, latest development and timely tips that make a great difference in getting a big break. In today's time the people who keep themselves updated through networking with people of different fields are in a unique position to take advantage by understanding the implications of these changes in the light of their own inherent strengths. Who knows even your passion or interest may become a great career or business opportunity at the point of inflection!

It may be difficult for you to keep yourself abreast in your career field itself, what to talk of other related fields and emerging career, where there may be a gold mine of opportunity waiting to be tapped. No wonder, many people who are well qualified, talented and sincere in their approach are not able to make the most of the upcoming opportunities simply because they are not aware of the new development and possible implications of these in the light of their own aptitude, interest and potential. At the same time there are many ordinary folks who get a dream career simply because they happen to be at the right place at the right time.

Do you often wonder how some people seem to break free from their past-career/job/place of stay so easily and get into new opportunities?

It is simply that -People who network are the people who go places.

Cutting edge actionable information is tacit

Just like the really valuable metal is hidden within raw ore, similarly the real cutting edge actionable information is always hidden within the formal systems and procedures of the organizations and institutions. This vital information cannot be extracted by reading manuals, going thorough the websites but it always require patient cultivation of informal network of friends and associates who alone can help you decipher the meaning and purpose behind the volumes of material.

The explicit knowledge in books, journals, and website cannot match the advantage of the tacit knowledge that comes through informal contacts and being part of network. In the context of career growth we can readily say that most of the actionable information is tacit. Information on the basis of which you can plan new and creative initiatives is always based on tacit experience of others. The following questions indicate your capacity to be connected to people, so as to be in a ready state to receive tacit knowledge about significant developments around you.

- Am I usually the first one (among my colleagues) to be able to get the relevant information that has significance for my work or area of interest?
- Am I usually involved in Team activities such as interesting and prestigious projects, which are storehouse of valuable knowledge and information for me?
- Am I usually aware of the moods and emotions of the people around me in work place or home etc?
- To what extent people seek quality information and suggestions from me on important professional matters
- To what extent I am able to seek quality information and suggestions from others on important professional matters

If the answer to the above questions is mostly positive, then chances are high that you are well connected to important sources of most tacit knowledge that matter. However if the answer to any of the question is "No", then it means that there is some scope for improving your support network. So let us first begin with a review of our support network.

Support Network Review

We need constant support and encouragement of other people for making the best of opportunities and planning our growth. The more diverse our support network the more we are able to generate the required support and resources in our favor.

The format in fig 10.1 describes the present sources of support and the specific type of support you need from each of

	Support Network	*Names*	*Type of support*	*Satisfaction Rating Low-1, Medium-2, High-3*
1.	Close friends/ Colleagues			
2.	Family members/ Relatives			
3.	Experts (professionals, trainers, consultants)			
4.	Social groups (profession, hobby club, sports, team, and so on)			
5.	Challengers or Competitors			
6.	Vendors/ suppliers			
7.	Gate Keepers (providers of access to someone or something desirable)			
8.	Almamater (batchmates, past colleagues, etc)			
9.	Assistants/Helpers			
10.	Financers (providers of funds)			
11.	Mentors (Seniors and teachers)			
12.	Any Other			

Fig 10.1 Support Network Review

them. It is possible that not all sources of support presently exist in your support network; consequently, some columns may be left blank. Also, the same provider may be listed more than once. In the satisfaction column, indicate your level of satisfaction with the support you presently receive from the corresponding source. Then complete the statements that follow the list.

Who all ask for my support and who can I depend for support...

____

____

____

The quality of my present support network is....

____

____

____

I use my support network most (when? How?)...

____

____

____

Support Network Improvement Plan

____

____

____

Select upto ten people who are current members of your support network and who can help you strengthen your support network from the perspective of career information and cutting edge information.

The main thing I would like to change about my support network is...

What are the unique strengths and resources of my key contacts...?

In what way my key contacts can help me in providing further contacts or critical information that may be useful and In what ways I can be useful to members of my support network.....?

In what additional ways can I use my support network?

Are there areas of mutual interest in which we may collaborate? In what ways we can collaborate for mutual benefits.

Full Circle on Career Growth & Joy at work

The people who make great and satisfying career for themselves and their loved ones are those who focus on leveraging their own inherent strength against the emerging opportunities. Rather than having a narrow focus, they maintain their flexibility to deploy their strengths in different types of fields and activities and often are pioneers in a new and emerging field. It is only natural that they are able to reap a lot of benefits of early movers. In fact if you look around yourself you will find a many great businesses are found on the principle of being the first one to make the most of a new opportunity.

Many of us pursue big dreams, which are often totally away from your current reality. This often leads to creating threatening situations in your current job or responsibilities etc. However the concept of generic project introduced by the author helps the reader in developing the flexibility to pursue new opportunities while continuing with their current occupation. Using the concept and exercises in your daily work, the reader can discover useful approaches for career growth and self development while working on their day to day jobs and activities. The concept of generic project thus provides a powerful tool from the perspective of current reality, while planning for future career growth.

The greatest possibilities lie at the horizon where your inner world meets the external world of dynamic change and emerging opportunities. Really smart people do not bother too much about their weakness, because they know that the foundations of great careers are based on the of twin pillars of our unique strengths (natural endowments) and the emerging opportunities of the external world. It is very much possible that a new development in some other field may lead to new possibilities in your field of interest also. For some it can mean "career metamorphosis", i.e reviving your old career and bringing in new passion and energy to your work.

It is the reflected wisdom that has greatest practical Value

How do we make things practical and useful to our immediate and urgent requirement? All books and resources can give concepts and ideas but it is ultimately how you codify these ideas in your own word and for your own world is what makes the real difference. This is what is shown in the cycle of passion below. This is the cycle of passion that we all need to discover for ourselves. We have to constantly review & reflect on our present approach to modify and develop our unique approach to career growth.

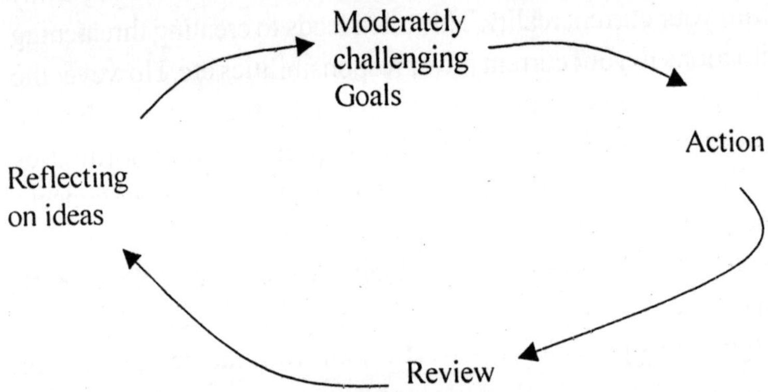

Fig. 10.2.

The cycle is important because our learning is complete and of practical use when we go through this cycle. How do you know whether you are moving forward in your career with this cycle?

Remember the excitement you had as a child when you first learn to ride bicycle. If you are getting the same excitement that you were getting as a child when learning to ride a bicycle, then know that you are moving in the right direct. When this path of career growth is traversed through the "cycle of passion" then career becomes the source of living with meaningful purpose, learning as well enjoyment. As you become adept with riding this cycle of passion, you develop tranquility of mind –a clam and quite mind in the midst of the chaos and cacophony of the modern world and such a mind would help you in taking better decisions about your self, career and life.

It is often said that it takes two to see one. So it will be a great idea If you share your learnings, aspiration etc with a trusted friend or well wisher. The more you share, the more you discuss the more you will be able to consolidate your learning and customize in ways that are more practical and rewarding to your specific requirement. As a trainer I have always known that it is the reader's reflected wisdom that has most practical value. So please do a favor by sending your valuable insight and reflections to me.

They say to me "you must choose between the pleasures of this world and the peace of the next world". And I say to them, "I have chosen both the delights of this world and the peace of the next world. For I know in my heart that the supreme poet wrote but one poem, and it scans perfectly, and it also rhymes perfectly.

Kahlil Gibran

Bibliography

List of Resources for facilitating career growth and joy at work

Finally, here is a list of additional resources -books, websites, journals etc which will be helpful in your quest for career growth and joy at work.

Books

1. Authentic Happiness by Martin Seligman, Nicholas Brealey Publishing, London 2003.

2. Flow: The Psychology of Happiness by Mihaly Csikszentmihalyi, Rider, London, 1992.

3. Art of happiness by Dalai Lama & Howard C Cutler, Mobius Easton Press, 1998.

4. Unlimited Power by Anthony Robbins, Pocket books, London 2001.

5. 07 Habits of highly effective people by Stephen R Covey, Simon & Schuster, 2004.

6. Now, Discover your strengths by Marcus Buckingham and Donald O. Clifton, Pocket books 2005.

7. Reclaiming the fire: How successful people overcome burnout by Dr Steven Berglas, Random house, 2001.

8. Women in Career and Life transition by Sandy Anderson, Jist Works, 1999.

9. Free to Succeed by Barbara Reinhold, Plume 2001.

10. You can heal yourself by Lousie Hay, Hay house 1984.

11. Mind Maps at Work by Tony Buzan, Harper Collins, London 2004.

12. The first 90 days: Critical success strategies for new leaders at all levels by Michael Watkins, Harvard business Press, Boston, 2003.

13. Critical thinking Strategies for decision making by Daniel A Feldman, Viva books, 2004.

14. Test Yourself.-Test your aptitude, personality and motivation and plan your career by Jim Barret, Kogan Pages India Pvt. Ltd, New Delhi, 2007.

15. Alternate Career choices by Usha Albuquerque & Amrit Sujan, Macmillan, 2004.

16. Inspiration, your ultimate calling by Dr Wayne W Dyer, hay house India Pvt. Ltd, Mumbai 2006.

17. Power up your mind. Learn faster, work smarter by Bill Lucas, Nicholas brearly publishing, 2001.

18. Job hunting in 21st Century: Exploding the myths, exploring the reality by carol A. Hacker, St. Lucie press, London,1999.

Career specific periodicals and websites

These career specific periodicals and websites are useful source of information about latest information on various career options that are emerging in the new economy. These are also useful source for accessing learning material and question banks for competitive exams and Interviews.

1. India Today, Aspire
2. Lakshya, (Hindi) Bhaskar group
3. Careers 360-Outlook group
4. Education World
5. Yuva
6. Life positive
7. www.educationtimes.com
8. www.winentrance.com
9. www.icscareeronline.com
10. www.ccdindia.com

Helpful Self Test sites

These web sites are useful for understanding your aptitude, discovering your strengths and general career guidance.

1. www.self-directed-search.com
2. www.careerkey.org
3. www.careerstorm.com
4. www.keirsey.com
5. www.vocerehab.com
6. www.strengthfinder.com

Helpful Websites –Universities/Institutions

These are useful websites of universities and institutions that are extremely helpful for planning your career and also provide access to useful self development and learning resources.

1. http; /www.cdm.uwaterloo.ca: This is a university of waterloo, US career service centre which provides excellent career resources both students and non students. Systematic steps to career planning are provided.

2. http; /www.bgsu.edu/offices/sa/career: This is a Bowling green state university, US career centre which provides excellent career resources both students and non students. Systematic steps to career planning are provided.

3. http; /www.rockportinstitue.com/pathfinder.php : Site also provides excellent career resources for deciding what career you should pursue.

4. www.princetonreviews.com/cte/quiz/default.asp

5. www.ibid.informindia.co.in: This is a website of newspaper and journals in India and also has information on industry verticals. This is a costly data base available with reputed institutes and libraries etc.

6. www.unjobs.com : This website provides details of the job opportunities in UN Jobs.

Job sites (General)

These are jobsites which are helpful in connecting you to prospective employers.

1. **www.monster.com**
2. **www.naukri.com**
3. **www.careerbuilder.com**
4. **www.hotjobs.com**
5. **www.indeed.com**

Job Site (top management)

1. **www.careerjournal.com**
2. **www.execunet.com**
3. **www.netshare.com**
4. **www.6figurejobs.com**

Job sites (Niche Listing)

1. **www.allretailjobs.com**
2. **wwwcallcentrejobs.com**

3. **www.nicheboards.com**
4. **www.telecomcareers.net**

Professional networking sites:

These are professional networking sites which would help you to network with fellow professionals and friends.

1. **www.linkedin.com**
2. **www.facebook.com**
3. **www.people.yahoo.com**

Index

T